THE PICNIC COOKBOOK

Barbara Weiland

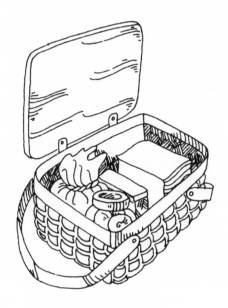

Butterick Publishing

ACKNOWLEDGMENTS

With a little help from my friends, the recipes in this book evolved through much testing, tasting and adjusting. My heartfelt thanks go to all those listed here (and to some, my deepest apologies for the pounds gained) for their help in ensuring that only the best of picnic foods found their way onto these pages. Their interest, generosity and willingness to contribute were greatly appreciated.

Marian Agazarian, Claire Albert, Suzanne Albrecht, Nancy Batal, Jane Battaglia, Ruth Ann Brooks, Barbara Campbell, Jean Christie, Diane Ciccarelli, Maggie and Carmen Corcimiglia, Kerry Courtice, Linda Cox, M. Diane Curl, Brad Daziel, Karen Horton Dillon, Sandy Elliott, Laura Fecych, Gayle Freer, Jeannie Glennon, Gail and Mark Heilmann, Jack and Barbara Lane, Irene Lundquist, Barbara McCormack, Joan McFarlane, Lenada Merrick, Jean Miller, Betsy Nilsen, Carol Oliphant, Jackie Oliveri, Pati Palmer, Bud and Sally Parker, Susy Pletsch, Peggy Poeppelmeier, Ann Roberts, Debra Roberts, Richard Roberts, Susan Rogers, Ron Smith, Todd Trevorrow, Terry Von Hightower, Margaret Ward and my mother, Eloise Weiland.

Book Design by Remo Cosentino

Photography by Victor Scocozzo

Illustrations by Elsie McCorkel

Library of Congress Cataloging in Publication Data

Weiland, Barbara.
 The picnic cookbook.

 Includes index.
 1. Cookery. 2. Outdoor cookery. 3. Picnicking.
4. Menus. I. Title.
TX823.W44   642'.3   78-24531
ISBN 0-88421-083-9

Manufactured and printed in the United States of America, published simultaneously in the USA and Canada.

DEDICATION

To Mom and Dad with love
and the deepest appreciation for your unfailing support
and encouragement in everything I do.

CONTENTS

MORE GOOD FOOD TO GO

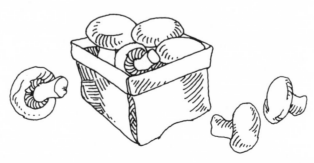

INTRODUCTION

For each individual, the word picnic probably evokes special, personal memories. For some it conjures up mental images of hot dogs cooked over an open fire high in the Rockies, for others a traditional Fourth of July family outing to a nearby park to watch the fireworks. The picnic I always remember first took place in my childhood, not that long ago, when my family and I shared a pasture with a herd of cows. Those cows were the nosiest animals on four legs and, as I remember it, we spent half of our lunchtime chasing them away from our picnic site under a shady tree. Forever after, the mere mention of "The Nosy Cow Picnic" brings back happy memories of family togetherness.

As an adult, I still think of picnics as special times for congeniality and good food. The simplest foods always taste better in a picnic atmosphere and food preparation for such occasions is somehow not the chore that routine meal-getting often becomes.

While the first dictionary definition of a picnic is "an outdoor party, usually held in the countryside, during which a meal is eaten," I prefer the broader definition—"an easy or pleasant time or experience"—in describing such meals. I firmly believe that picnicking is a state of mind and picnic meals can be enjoyed throughout the seasons in all kinds of settings, indoors as well as out. While some of the most beautiful "dining rooms" in any city are its well-kept parks, they are only one of the many wonderful places for enjoying the camaraderie of informal dining. Don't overlook the possibility of enjoying a picnic brunch in bed on a blustery cold day. And never let bad weather alter picnic plans, even if you must ultimately move indoors. Congenial company and a hamper full of good food can go a long way toward redeeming a gloomy day. Why not plan a rainy-day indoor picnic for restless little ones when it's already been raining for days and the long-range forecast is for more of the same? The prospect of a "picnic" will surely brighten their spirits—and yours—even though you can't eat outdoors. With a little imagination, you'll be able to dream up many more reasons for picnicking than I have provided in the pages of this book.

Whether you buy your picnic lunch at the deli counter, cook it over the coals of a glowing fire, spread it out on a cloth in a honey-scented field of fresh-mown hay, or stop along the roadside to eat gypsy-style, I'm sure you will agree that there are few culinary pleasures in life—summer, winter, spring or fall—that can compare to a picnic meal. Planning such meals is a very personalized activity and although much thought went into organizing the picnic menus included in this book, I know you will find yourself doing lots of mixing and matching to come up with menus all your own. Don't be afraid to swap recipes in the menus or to make substitutions from the "Mix and Match Recipes" chapter at the end of the book. The menus are simply suggestions meant to stimulate your culinary creativity. (The recipe for each menu entry marked with an asterisk is given in the following section or on the page indicated. Recipes for such basics as pastry and mayonnaise are gathered in Part III.)

The dishes described in this book are particularly well suited for packing up to take wherever your feet lead—by a mountain stream, under the stars, in a foliage-strewn, ancient graveyard, on the steps of your favorite museum or library, in front of a roaring fire in your own family or living room, on a snowy hillside. In addition, scattered throughout are picnic menus featuring interesting and tasty foreign foods to add to your expanding picnic recipe collection. As a nation, our increased exposure to the other countries of the world has heightened our awareness of foreign food customs, giving us many new options for picnic foods besides the traditional potato salad, baked beans and hot dogs that were standard fare when I was a child. These still have a place in anyone's repertoire, but they shouldn't be the only foods offered family and friends at picnic gatherings.

This book is not devoted to the art of outdoor cookery in which entire meals are cooked in any one of the growing number of outdoor grills, including the backyard gas and electric models. The assumption is made that picnics are primarily prepared ahead of time, and some outdoor cooking might be used on occasion to prepare one or two dishes or to warm already prepared foods. Further information on outdoor cookery, including backpack cooking, can be found in any one of a large number of books on the subject.

Food shared with good friends in the open air is an unbeatable combination, so pack up some "good food to go" and enjoy a picnic meal wherever and whenever the spirit moves you!

PICNIC PRELIMINARIES

The Picnic Basket

Accessories and Supplies

Careful choice of equipment for preparing and packing picnic foods as well as serving them will contribute to the many happy memories of your special meals enjoyed outdoors, as well as those forced or purposely planned for indoors. In 1896, a food-writer made the following observation about picnic-giving in a popular women's magazine of the time. Her thoughts are as appropriate today as when she penned them.

Although all picnickers should expect to endure many little inconveniences without complaint and should be willing sometimes to use fingers in place of knives and forks, they should *not* be compelled to eat a luncheon composed of foods that have their original flavors impaired or wholly changed by too close contact with one another. It is a small matter to see a harmless spider or a large black cat promenading across the table-cloth, but the spirit of a true philosopher is needed if one is to bear with equanimity the discovery that the sandwiches taste hopelessly of the bananas and the fried chicken of the cake. After you have prepared a charming luncheon, fair hostess [or host], see to it that the viands are properly packed, and then the success of your picnic will be assured.

Day Entertainments and Other Functions, September, 1896

This chapter contains many suggestions for accessories and supplies for outfitting your picnic hamper, keeping foods hot or cold, and for cooking on the spot. Included here are suggestions for recycling everyday throwaways for picnic service. Recommendations for items basic to all picnic baskets follow along with discussions of equipment that are arranged alphabetically under the following categories: Carrying the Meal; Keeping Food Hot or Cold; Setting the Picnic "Table"; Cooking Out; Picnic First Aid. In conjunction with this information, don't neglect the following chapter on food and fire safety to refresh your memory on how to avoid food poisoning and to use fire safely and wisely when preparing picnic foods.

The Basic Basket

Inveterate picnickers know the value of keeping a picnic basket always supplied with all the incidentals that amateurs spend time rounding up when the sudden urge or invitation to enjoy an outdoor meal finds them unprepared. With a basic basket, it's as simple as 1-2-3 to add the feast and go, rather than hunting for all those things you would normally forget in the rush of a spur-of-the-moment picnic. I have a friend who has not one but four picnic baskets always outfitted for last-minute adventures. One will suffice for most households, especially if you carefully plan the contents to meet your specific needs and vow to use the contents *only* for picnics.

The "basic basket" need not be a basket at all. In addition to all the baskets and basket alternatives discussed below, one of the simplest and least expensive ways to store and carry picnic gear is in a cardboard file storage box available at office supply stores and many variety discount stores. Some are available in bright colors and the plain brown models can be easily brightened with the addition of colorful adhesive-backed vinyl or a pretty printed fabric to match your picnic tablecloth. Apply fabric with white glue or wallpaper paste and give it a coat or two of clear varnish for a stain-resistant, wipe-clean finish. Line the inside with the adhesive vinyl, too, for easy cleanup and longer wear. Fill the box with your picnic gear and store on a closet shelf in a clean, dry place.

Whether you use a box or a basket, be sure to replace used items when you return from a picnic or you will eventually defeat the purpose of keeping a "basic basket."

The following is a table of indispensable items, necessary for all but the simplest picnic meals. Starred (*) items are treated in further detail in the following pages. If expense is no object, the supplies listed here can be the very best you can afford as long as they are easily portable, a judgment only you can make. Otherwise, don't be afraid to recycle kitchen containers, plastic bags, etc. for use in your supply kit. Paper, plastic and foam products are suitable for many picnic foods. Beware of flimsy utensils, especially those made of lightweight plastics, a poor investment because they crack easily.

Carrying the Meal

Baskets and Basket Alternatives. The traditional hardwood splint picnic basket with hinged lid and swinging handles is no longer your only choice when it comes to picnic carriers. Baskets abound in every imaginable size and shape and can be found at import shops, specialty stores and even in the home furnishings and accessories sections of department stores. You might find unique styles at antique stores and flea markets. Baskets range in price from inexpensive versions to elaborate wicker models outfitted

BASIC PICNIC SUPPLIES

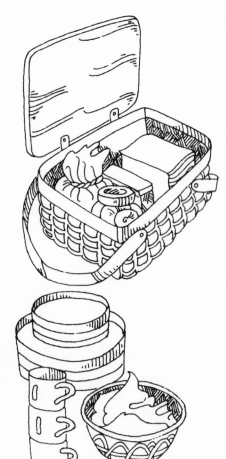

Eating Utensils

dinnerware, glasses, mugs*

flatware and serving pieces*

tablecloth or ground cloth and napkins*; placemats optional*

plastic tablecloth to cover picnic foods in case of a sudden rainstorm

Serving Equipment

can opener

corkscrew

sharp knife in a protective sheath (at least one)

Swiss Army knife*

small carving board for slicing bread, meat and cheese, for sandwich-making, and to use as a trivet when necessary

soup ladle or scoop

small airtight plastic food containers*

Gerry tubes for condiments*

small thermal containers and a large jug*

Cooking Equipment

fireplace matches

fire starter*

plastic sprinkler or spray bottle to put out fires or cooking flareups

small portable grill*

lightweight cookware or an all-purpose skillet*

cooking utensils and skewers*

pot holders, asbestos mitt

Staples

closable salt and pepper shakers, or standard shakers with holes covered with masking tape to prevent spilling

sugar in packets in an airtight plastic container

water jug to fill at the last minute*

Cleanup

sponge or washcloth in small plastic container

premoistened towelettes

paper towels

small roll heavy-duty aluminum foil

small roll transparent wrap

package of small plastic bags and wire closures

large plastic garbage bags, some for trash and some for picnic "treasures"

whisk broom for cleaning picnic tables and benches before and after use

Safety Equipment

first-aid kit*

flashlight

Niceties (not at all necessary)

inexpensive bud vase for wildflowers in spring and summer, dried weeds and grasses in fall and winter

candles and candle-holders

wine carafe

with plastic dinnerware, flatware, and thermal and plastic containers. You can probably outfit your own large suitcase-style wicker basket with inexpensive but sturdy equipment for much less than you would pay for a preassembled basket and utensils. Those that I've examined are extremely expensive and contain flimsy, easily broken plastic dining service and implements.

Also consider putting decorative baskets in your home into temporary service for picnics. Bushel baskets and wicker laundry baskets are also possible candidates. Line them with large, colorful tablecloths which can be folded over the contents. Of course, most baskets won't keep foods cold or hot, so they are best used to carry eating utensils and place settings, serving equipment, napkins and tablecloth or ground cloth, and foods that don't require insulation.

Wooden mushroom baskets make wonderful lunch baskets lined with bright tissue paper or an oversize napkin or dish towel. They're just large enough to hold a fine meal for one or maybe two, depending on the appetites. You'll find mushroom baskets at the produce market, but unless you buy the whole basket (that's a lot of mushrooms), you will probably have to ask the produce manager to save empties for you. If you know someone who works at a restaurant that serves mushrooms, ask your friend to save the baskets for you. Large wooden berry baskets can also be used in this manner but they generally lack the convenient handle that characterizes mushroom baskets.

If you plan to include a large tossed salad in your picnic, outfit a round basket—a bushel type or something more decorative—to hold the greens and keep them chilled until serving time. Place greens in a large covered container that will fit loosely in your basket. Then line the basket with a heavy plastic garbage bag, place a layer of cracked ice in the bottom, insert the salad container and pack more ice around it. Carefully add a small, tightly covered jar of salad dressing to the salad greens, then cover tightly. If there's room in the basket, stack salad plates on top of the covered greens. Of course, this idea works for keeping other foods chilled as well. Round baskets lined with layers of newspaper will help keep hot foods hot. Wrap casseroles containing foods like baked beans in heavy-duty foil, then tuck them into the newspaper-lined basket, and cover them with more newspapers and finally a towel or tablecloth.

Slabs of polyurethane foam, often available in fabric stores for making chair cushions, have good insulating qualities and can be used to line wicker baskets to help keep foods cold. Cut 1-inch-thick pieces of foam to line the top, bottom and sides of your basket and glue them in place with white glue. Add thoroughly chilled foods and bottles of wine or cans of soda, and close the basket

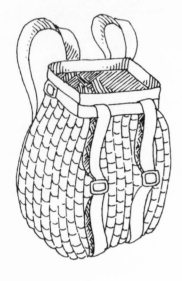

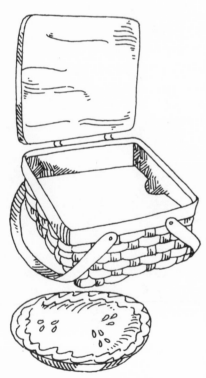

tightly. With the basket in the shade, the contents will stay cool up to four hours.

Don't neglect small baskets for use as serving containers for finger foods. They're attractive, lightweight and are often available in nested sets, which makes carrying them a cinch.

Each of the following items has merit as a possible carrier for picnic food.

Backpack Basket. Shaped to lie against your back and equipped with an adjustable harness, this large basket is especially good for carrying breakables as well as bulky, odd-shaped items.

Canvas Totes. You'll find these roomy bags at sailing shops and sporting goods stores. They're made of heavy canvas, usually with a reinforced bottom and sturdy handles.

Fishing Creels. Fishing creels can carry more than fish, and that includes your picnic lunch. They're available at sporting goods stores in several styles.

Hardware Caddies and Carpenters' Boxes. These make sturdy carryalls for bottles and jars. Check your hardware store for them.

Pie Carrier. This is a special basket shaped to hold a 9-inch pie level under a removable interior rack, leaving additional space for packing another pie, a cake or other picnic foods. The size is about 12 × 10 × 7 inches deep. Pie carriers are easy to decorate since the lids are usually plywood. Try stenciling or tole painting a design on the lid, doing the same on a picnic hamper for a matching set.

Covered cake and pie carriers are also available in airtight plastic versions, somehow not as appealing as the wooden style, but certainly as effective.

Plastic Laundry Baskets. These baskets are usually available in bright crayon colors and in several styles. The sides are made in an open webbing design with handles on top and a solid plastic bottom. The smaller size, about 12 × 20 inches, will hold lunch for one and beach gear, too.

Rucksack. Small, lightweight knapsacks are ideal for carrying lunch on your back for hiking, skiing and biking picnics.

Suitcase. Tucked away in the back closet or the garage is probably an old suitcase that's outdated or slightly damaged but not shabby enough to throw away. Don't overlook it as a possible picnic carrier. It can be outfitted with your special picnic equipment—dinnerware, flatware, tablecloth, napkins, barbecue set—always packed and ready to go at a moment's notice. Due to the manner in which a suitcase is carried, it won't make a good food carrier, though. If your suitcase is a little shabby looking, you could dress it up with a coat of brightly printed fabric, inside and out. If you don't have an old suitcase, keep a lookout for a suitable one at tag or yard sales, thrift shops and antique stores. And don't forget about those inexpensive vinyl-lined fabric suitcases readily available at variety and discount stores.

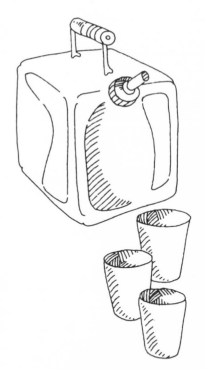

Carrying food inside the picnic basket can pose some problems if you're not aware of some of the following alternatives.

Folding Water Jug. A compact polyethylene jug that folds for storage and packing is a handy picnic item because it eliminates the need for carrying drinking water from home if you will be picnicking near a fresh-water source. The jug is equipped with a spigot for easy dispensing and it imparts no aftertaste or odor. Of course, it can also be used to transport liquids other than water. It can also be used to freeze water for a convenient refrigerant for coolers (see page 16). Used in this manner, the coolant will last longer than ice cubes, prevent water accumulation in the cooler and provide refreshing ice water as the ice melts. Folding jugs are normally available at sporting goods stores in 2½- and 5-gallon capacities.

Food Containers and Serving Dishes. A wide array of attractive airtight plastic containers is available for packing picnic food. Many of these products are so attractive that they can easily double as serving dishes straight from the cooler or hamper to the table. In addition, don't overlook the possibility of recycling small plastic containers like those used for margarine or butter as well as foods purchased in a delicatessen. I keep a good supply of these in my picnic supply box to take along for leftovers. They're also handy at picnic time for holding sauces, dips and individual servings of desserts, crackers, even small salads.

Gerry Tubes. Backpackers find these little plastic food-storage containers indispensable and so will serious picnickers. Shaped like a large open-ended toothpaste tube, each container is filled from the bottom with such foods as ketchup, jam, honey or peanut butter. When filled, the bottom is folded over and closed with the clip provided. To use, the screw-on cap is removed and the contents are squeezed out, just like toothpaste. The tubes are lightweight and easily refilled, making it unnecessary to carry along heavy glass containers of these foods. Check for them at sporting goods stores.

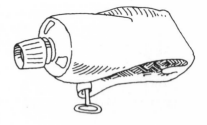

Wineskin. Traditionally made of natural leather lined with rubber, wineskins are now available in a leather-wrapped plastic version as well. They are specially shaped to aid in drinking liquid

without a cup or glass, and are most often carried around the neck on a cord by skiers and backpackers. Usual capacity is 1 liter. Some people refer to these as bota bags in reference to their Basque origin.

Keeping Food Hot or Cold

Coolers (Ice Chests). Picnic coolers are indispensable for keeping cold foods cold, especially those containing meat, fish, eggs or dairy products. Coolers are available in a wide variety of sizes and shapes at several price levels. Their insulating qualities vary and can be augmented with the use of ice blocks, crushed ice or ice substitutes (see page 17). Coolers made of lightweight but sturdy plastics have generally replaced the heavier enameled steel cases, but these are still available and advisable for heavy loads and large amounts of food. Some of the lightweight chests are sturdy enough to use as seating and some are available with seat cushions. Others have detachable lids which double as beverage trays, and some are fitted with removable food trays and cutting boards. Handles often double as bottle openers. Look for a cooler with a leakproof drain.

Before you invest in an ice chest, analyze your needs and available storage space. One of the lightweight styrofoam chests may be all you really need if your picnics are sporadic and normally a short distance from home base. If picnicking is a way of life for you and your family, especially in the summer, then consider the cooler an investment and buy the best you can afford. Use insulated picnic jugs and containers (page 17) to supplement the space in your cooler when necessary.

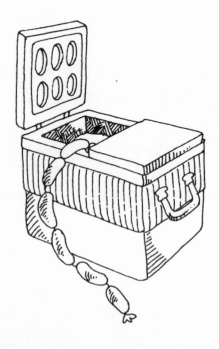

For best results with plastic coolers, prechill the interior by allowing the chest to stand with ice and cold water in it for at least 15 minutes. After prechilling, drain, then use ice cubes or blocks, cracked ice, artificial refrigerant (see ice substitutes, below) or dry ice to keep contents cold. (Handle dry ice with care to avoid skin burns. Wrap it in heavy paper before placing it in the cooler on top of the foods to be kept cold.) Use plenty of ice and nest bottled and canned goods in the ice, covering them as much as possible. Place perishables such as dairy products (in containers) and packaged meats directly on the ice for optimum cooling. Don't overstock the cooler; air circulation is necessary to keep temperatures low. While in use, keep the cooler away from the direct rays of the sun if possible, and keep it closed as much as possible to maintain cold temperatures. If shade is not available, cover the cooler with canvas or newspaper.

After each use, clean the interior of the cooler with hot water and mild soap and rinse it with clear, warm water. Allow it to dry thoroughly and store it with the cover propped open to avoid the buildup of stale odors and mildew. Be sure to rinse it again thoroughly before the next use to remove any dust or dirt.

Ice Substitutes. Commercially available gels in compact plastic containers provide cooling for picnic foods when properly used. These "blocks of ice" are inexpensive, reusable and nontoxic. They must be placed in a freezer for five to eight hours before using them in any of the available coolers. The cooling action lasts for several hours. Blocks are available in several sizes at variety, grocery and hardware stores as well as at sporting goods outlets. It's a good idea to keep a block or two in the freezer to pack those last-minute picnics.

If you plan to include a picnic punch made from frozen fruit concentrates and you're short on ice, consider packing the frozen juices in their cans as an ice substitute. Put sugar and other necessary ingredients for the punch in a picnic jug (see below) and mix the drink after you arrive at your destination. Discarded milk cartons filled not quite full with water or juice and then frozen make good blocks of "ice," too.

Refrigerator Bags. If limited storage space is a consideration in choosing picnic equipment, you might want to use refrigerator bags for foods that should be kept cold or warm. These light-weight, waterproof bags are made of vinyl insulated with fiber-glass, and close with a zipper. They come in several sizes. Food should be preheated or prechilled before being placed in these bags. Hot foods will drop in temperature, so they should be slightly overheated to allow for the temperature drop. They should also be wrapped in paper or aluminum foil to avoid sticking to the vinyl lining.

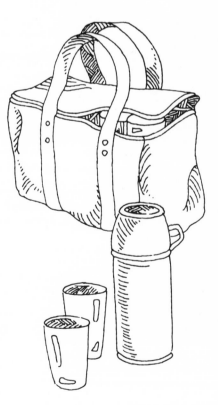

Refrigerator bags will keep cold foods cold approximately six to eight hours and warm foods warm approximately four to six hours. If you use ice, be sure to put it in a waterproof container before placing it in the bag, as leakage might be a problem. Obviously, hot and cold foods cannot be stored in the same bag.

Thermal Containers. With the advent and improvement of plas-tics, there are now thermal containers to meet a wide range of picnic needs. These containers are constructed with either a vacuum or a layer of polyurethane between the inner lining and the outer wall. This insulates the contents so that they retain their temperatures during storage. Thermal bottles in sizes from pint to

quart to gallon capacities are available in steel and plastic constructions. (Some inner linings are glass.) The plastic, of course, is
comparatively lightweight, but some people object to it because
they feel it imparts a "plastic" taste to the foods—something I've
never experienced in using these containers.

Thermal picnic jugs with wide mouths and faucets for easy
serving are meant to carry prepared hot or cold beverages. Some
are available with pour spouts as well. The wide mouth allows easy
filling and, if necessary, easy serving from the top.

For optimum insulation, it is always wise to preheat or prechill
thermal containers before filling them with food or beverages.
Simply fill a container with boiling water to preheat it or with ice
water to chill, then cap it tightly and let it stand while you prepare
the food. If you prepare foods that are to be chilled the day before
your outing, pack them in containers and place them in the
refrigerator with the lids on but not screwed shut. Close the
containers tightly after the food has had time to chill through and
leave them in the refrigerator until you are ready to depart. Be
sure to clean thermal containers after each use and to store them
with the lids unscrewed. Never use sharp objects in plastic or glass
containers as a puncture will destroy the insulating qualities and
cause leakage into the vacuum. In general, thermal containers will
keep food warm above 140°F or cold below 40°F.

In addition, don't overlook ice buckets already on hand as
possible picnic containers. Partially fill the bucket with cracked ice
and insert a smaller container of food or beverage down in the ice.
Cover with ice and the lid. The ice can later be used in your picnic
beverage.

Setting the Picnic "Table"

Flatware. Although throwaway plastic flatware is readily available, lightweight and inexpensive, I can't think of anyone who
really enjoys using it, other than small children who like its
novelty. There is really no excuse for knives that don't cut, forks
with broken tines and spoons that melt in your soup! Department
stores run periodic "special sales" on attractive stainless steel
flatware, and the prices warrant buying a service for eight in a
simple pattern to tuck away with your other picnic gear. Sometimes matching serving pieces are also specially priced. Your
guests will certainly appreciate your thoughtfulness in providing
utensils that don't interfere with their dining enjoyment.

Of course, the plastic flatware has its place, particularly when a
heavy picnic basket cannot be carried on a long hike or on a

camping trip where washing facilities are not always available. Then, too, sturdier plastic flatware can be purchased at a higher price, which might make you consider washing and storing the utensils for reuse. If space is a problem in a backpack, check sporting goods stores for eating utensils that fold compactly to fit in the nooks and crannies of the pack.

Carrying flatware in the picnic basket can be simplified by wrapping it in colorful dish towels tied with bright ribbons, or by placing it in recycled cylindrical tennis ball or potato chip cans. Cover these cans with bright adhesive-backed vinyl or fabric to match your picnic accessories.

Ground Cloths and Tablecloths. A bright tablecloth might be all you want or need to set off your picnic meal. When tables are unavailable, you might need a cloth with the dual purpose of providing a place to eat and of protecting picnickers from the damp ground. Ground cloths can be purchased at sporting goods stores but it's easy to improvise more attractive ones. A quilted bedspread that has seen better days on your bed provides a little padding when spread on the hard ground. Or, make a new quilted cloth from any of the double-faced quilted fabrics available by the yard. They're normally 40 to 45 inches in width, so buy about 2½ yards and bind the raw edges in a contrasting bias tape or braid. Use a coordinating print or plain fabric for napkins. Of course, you can always spread this on a picnic table, too.

Another ground cloth that's comfortable and easy-care can be made from those inexpensive woven scatter rugs found in discount department stores, supermarkets and some drugstores. Buy several and whipstitch them together, patchwork fashion, using heavy cord and a tapestry needle. To make matching cushions, fold extra rugs in half crosswise, whipstitch two of the three open sides together, and stuff with polyester fiberfill or a pillow form. Finish by whipstitching the remaining edges together. This picnic ground cloth with cushions can do double duty as a beach mat and pillows. Since sand sifts through the weave, the whole thing can be washed in your washing machine (depending on how large you make it).

Flannel-backed vinyls printed in bold designs make great cloths. They're available by the yard and are usually wider than average fabrics. Brightly printed flat sheets are also tablecloth alternatives, with matching napkins made from pillowcases. Even a vinyl or rubber-backed shower curtain can double as a picnic tablecloth. For a comfy, absorbent, easily laundered tablecloth, seam together large fluffy bath towels. Washcloths make great picnic napkins, too. Last but not least, don't overlook painters' canvas drop cloths. They're sturdy and not too expensive, and you'll find them at paint stores, of course. If you're feeling creative, paint a bold design on the cloth with acrylic paints or try your hand at stenciling.

Windy-day picnics are a common occurrence, so to keep the picnic tablecloth from flapping in the breeze and upsetting the table, use one of the following methods:

1. Spread the cloth on the table, then tie each corner into a self-knot.

2. Encase two or three drapery weights in a small square of fabric. Hand sew a weighted square on the underside of each corner of the tablecloth.

3. If you are making a picnic cloth, sew a triangular pocket on the wrong side of each corner, leaving the top open. After the cloth is spread on the table, fill the pockets with a handful of small stones.

4. Attach Velcro cut in circles or strips to the underside of the tablecloth at each corner. To position the Velcro, spread the cloth on a large rectangular table or your backyard picnic table and mark the position of the fold at each corner. When using the cloth on a table, press the pieces of Velcro together to keep the corners in position. When used as a ground cloth, the Velcro will not show.

Picnic Tables. While picnic tables are convenient to use, they are often missing from your chosen site. If you must have a table you can always take along your card table and chairs, a lot to carry for a fuss-free meal. Better yet, take only the card table, an old one or a rummage sale find, with the legs cut down to make chairs unnecessary. Sit on cushions or folded terry cloth towels placed on the ground. This makes a particularly pleasant arrangement for beach picnics, where sand seems to get into everything you spread on the beach blanket.

Place Mats. Place mats are a dispensable item in your picnic basket; but since you never know what you will find on picnic benches, you might take along washable or vinyl place mats to use on the bench instead of the table.

Place Settings. Picnic place settings can range all the way from flimsy paper plates to lightweight plastic dinnerware to your best china. Easy portability and cleanup are usually the major considerations for most picnickers. Some picnics, which consist of sandwiches and finger foods, demand no serving plates or place settings or, at most, call for a paper plate or bowl. Others can be so elaborate that half the kitchen must be transported to the dining site. If you plan a picnic at home, your everyday place settings are suitable, but you might want to invest in a set of brightly colored plastic place settings and serving dishes to store away in your picnic supply basket. Offerings are varied in a wide price range. Look for dishes that stack easily and compactly and are break resistant. Avoid flimsy plastics which are easily cracked. Nested place settings are available for serious backpackers. They are small and lightweight and are easily tucked into small spaces in backpacks, but they are not especially attractive and don't add much eye appeal to outdoor meals.

Paper dinnerware is also available in a wide range of shapes and sizes as well as prints and colors. Although it is relatively inexpensive and easily disposable if you happen to be using a campfire, it is often inadequate for juicy or hot, runny foods like baked beans. If you do use paper products, choose one of the sturdier constructions divided into segments to prevent foods from running into each other on the plate. Somehow the segments are never large enough, though, to accommodate the giant helpings that picnickers seem to require when they encounter food in the open air, so take along an extra large supply of plates. Paper dinnerware is by far the most easily portable since it is so lightweight and you usually don't have to carry it home again. When picnic plans call for do-it-yourself meals like the Salad Bar (page 105), paper bowls are probably the best choice for setting out the ingredients.

It is also possible to recycle food trays from your kitchen for picnic meals. Save the colorful styrofoam trays on which fruits and vegetables as well as many meats are now packaged. They can be used for packing and serving individual portions of finger foods, sandwiches and simple desserts as well as individual colorful antipasto salads. Wash the trays with warm, soapy water, rinse and dry them, and store them with your other picnic supplies. When ready to use, fill the trays with individual food portions and wrap them securely with transparent wrap. The trays are easy to stack in a picnic cooler and make buffet-style picnic dining marvelously simple. The trays can be reused several times.

Drinking glasses, cups and mugs are also available in brightly colored plastics but when space and weight are a problem, use paper cups. If your picnic includes hot *and* cold beverages, buy the paper cups marked "suitable for hot beverages" and use them for both. Never try to serve hot foods in waxed, paper cups. The wax will melt and the cups collapse. If space allows, take along your silver wine goblets, pewter cups—even the crystal if it's a special occasion and packing and carrying are not problems.

Insulated foam plastic cups can also be used for soups, but consider using Japanese rice bowls as a pretty alternative.

Cooking Out

For those who enjoy the challenge of campfire cooking and who think food tastes better when cooked outdoors, stoves, ovens and grills abound. Many of them are particularly well suited for backpackers and hikers who demand lightweight but functional cooking tools. Check hardware stores, large department stores and sporting goods stores to locate the outdoor cooking pieces you feel you'll need. On occasion, traditional kitchen equipment can be pressed into outdoor service.

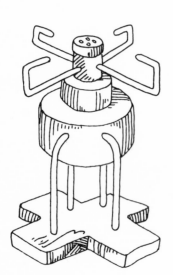

Campstoves. Campstoves will never replace the campfire and the taste its coals lend to grilled steaks and hot dogs. Unfortunately, however, campfires are fast becoming a thing of the past for safety reasons as well as for the simple fact that wood to feed such fires is becoming increasingly scarce as more and more people head for the wilds to "get away from it all" every weekend. It is still possible to cook outdoors, however, using one of a variety of campstoves. These leave no fire scars on natural settings, provide a reliable source of heat and, most importantly, can be instantly turned off and so prevent forest fires.

Small campstoves, designed for backpackers and hikers, have only one cooking surface, so preparation of more than one hot food must be carefully planned and timed. The most commonly used stoves are the white gas, kerosene, propane and butane cartridge powered models. Other fuels include alcohol and jellied alcohol which is most commonly known as sterno. Each has advantages and drawbacks as outlined in the chart that follows.

Charcoal Briquettes. Charcoal briquettes can be purchased in 10- and 25-pound bags and of all charcoal, they provide the most uniform, long-lasting and reliable fires for outdoor grilling. Sometimes difficult to start, they might require a helping hand from a liquid or solid fire starter. See page 32 for directions on how to start a charcoal-fueled fire.

Cooking and Serving Utensils. Cooking and serving utensils are easily found in sets containing a wide spatula with slots for draining fats and juices, a meat skewer, tongs for lifting and turning meats and retrieving foil-wrapped potatoes and corn from hot coals, tongs for shifting hot coals, a fork and sometimes a sharp knife. A long-handled brush with firm, stiff bristles for basting is helpful, too. Be sure to look for a set with long handles to avoid unnecessary contact with heat and flames from the cooking fire. To save burned fingers and toasted faces, don't try to substitute your kitchen utensils for this equipment as the handles

COMPARISON OF FUEL SOURCES FOR PICNIC-CAMPING STOVES

Fuel	Advantages	Drawbacks
alcohol	■ nonexplosive ■ relatively nontoxic ■ relatively available ■ odorless	■ takes three times as long to cook as gas
butane cartridge	■ easiest to use: priming and pumping unnecessary, simply lit with a match	■ can be explosive if incorrectly handled ■ stove must remain assembled until the cartridge is empty; might make packing difficult ■ more expensive and not refillable ■ slow to put out heat ■ cartridge is heavier than kerosene or gas ■ cartridge is under pressure and could leak ■ cannot be used below freezing or at high altitudes
kerosene	■ less volatile and less dangerous than white gas ■ readily available	■ some skill needed to start the fuel; requires pumping ■ gives off smoke and noxious odor ■ requires special spun-aluminum bottle with gasketed screw-top to carry ■ no control valve
propane	■ stoves are small and lightweight	■ doesn't work as well as gas in cold weather ■ propane cylinders are heavy
jellied alcohol	■ safe and inexpensive ■ easily portable ■ easily extinguished ■ ideal for precooked foods that should be kept warm at the table	■ burns less intensely than other fuels ■ impossible to control heat, so food takes longer to heat
white gas	■ no special priming fuel needed ■ once lit, fire needs no further pumping ■ readily available ■ stoves are small and lightweight	■ combustible; will explode if stove is filled while hot ■ requires special spun-aluminum bottle with gasketed screw-top to carry

will be too short to safely work over a hot fire. Handles should range in length from 10 to 15 inches to assure safety; handles of all metal utensils should end in a wooden or plastic grip which will not conduct heat.

Cookware. Almost anyone who has done any outdoor cooking over an open fire will agree that cast-iron cooking utensils are the best choice. But they *are* heavy and therefore difficult to transport. Lightweight aluminum cook sets are a second choice. If you cannot carry a cast-iron skillet, substitute a 10½-inch, 14-gauge steel skillet with a long handle. Look for one with a detachable handle to make packing easier. The steel skillet will not be quite as heavy as the cast-iron one and will give almost equal results. It is important to wipe it clean and dry after each use or it will rust.

If you don't plan to do much outdoor cooking, you can always use your everyday cookware, but be prepared for sooty, black bottoms and lost lids. Better still, improvise with kitchen cast-aways. Save empty 1-, 2- and 3-pound coffee cans (they nest easily), and when you plan to cook out, take the cans and tongs or pliers to use as a lifter. Line each can with a large piece of heavy-duty foil and leave long ends protruding above the can to aid in lifting out cooked foods. When the cans become very blackened, simply discard them and replace them with new ones. If you need to cover what is cooking in one of these improvised "pots," place a square of aluminum foil over the can and secure it with string or a rubber band. Steamed puddings or breads are especially well suited to this improvised cooking utensil. (See page 177 for Steamed Cranberry Pudding.)

If space is limited for packing cookware, buy a good skillet. You can use it to boil, broil, simmer, poach, stew, even make coffee and boil water for tea if necessary.

If you would prefer not to carry along pots and pans, it is possible to make disposable pans from heavy-duty aluminum foil using the following procedure.

1. Use two layers of foil for a pan. Cut foil pieces several inches larger all around than the finished pan.

2. On all four edges of the foil sheet (two layers), turn in 2 inches as shown. Fold in the short ends first, then the long ends.

3. Turn folded foil over to other side and use your fingernail to score the foil all the way around 1 inch from the edge. Score through corners as shown.

4. Fold edges up on scoring. Pinch corners, then fold them back against the sides of the "pan."

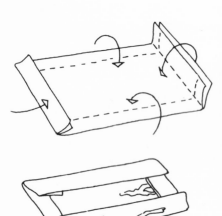
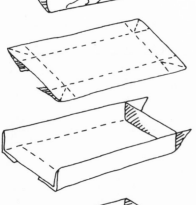
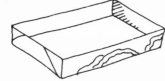

Fire Starter. Commercially prepared fire ribbon, tablets or solid cakes are designed to aid in starting fires in place of tinder (page 35). Leftover candle stubs or small birthday cake candles serve the purpose, too. You can make your own fire starter by recycling newspapers. Roll 12-inch squares of old newspapers into solid sticks and tie them securely with cord. Then dip the sticks into hot, melted paraffin until they are saturated with wax. Allow them to dry, then cut them into ½-inch cylinders.

Liquid fire starters such as lighter fluid are most often used to start charcoal fires. They are combustible and must be used with caution. Follow the directions on the can for use and storage. Never spray lighter fluid on live coals and never use gasoline or alcohol as a fire starter.

You can also use the twigs from your yard to prepare a fire starter. In the fall as you rake the leaves, save small dry branches and sticks. Tie them in small bundles and place the bundles in small paper bags. Tape the bags with masking tape and store them in a dry place for free, ever-ready, easily transported fire starters.

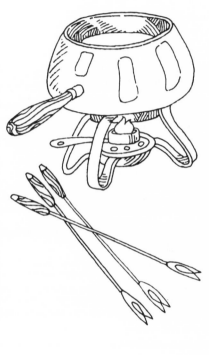

Fondue Pot. Sometimes it's nice to serve hot food at a picnic without the bother of fire building or carrying along the hibachi and all the necessary cooking equipment. The fondue pot is a good alternative. It is relatively small and easy to pack with your other picnic gear, and can be used to cook fondue or to reheat a dessert, melt butter or make a sauce for something on the menu. If you plan to use the fondue pot for picnic purposes, choose one of enamel over cast iron or steel rather than a lightweight aluminum model which is really not suitable for heavy cheese or chocolate sauces. The fondue pot sits on a stand which holds a fuel source, the best of which is an alcohol burner. Many use jellied alcohol. While this is an inexpensive, safe and easily portable heat source for fondue pots, it burns less intensely than alcohol-fueled burners, the food takes longer to cook and it is not possible to regulate the heat. It is the ideal fuel to use for foods cooked at home, carried to the picnic in a thermal container and kept warm at the picnic. If you plan to make the fondue at the picnic, an alcohol-fueled burner is the best choice since the heat can be regulated and sauces and broths can be brought to a simmer or boil if desired. Don't forget to pack sharp, long-handled fondue forks.

Grills. Portable grills come in styles to suit a variety of needs. Some are knockdown and fitted with a pan to hold charcoal. Others are made to hold cooking utensils over open fires and have legs that fold against the grid for easy packing and storage. These models are lightweight and relatively small, for backpacking. If

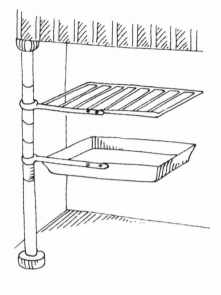

weight and space are no problem, recycle an old refrigerator or oven rack for grilling—they are larger and sturdier than the portable varieties.

Fireplace grills are also an alternative for indoor and outdoor use. These are adjustable grills that fit any fireplace. They usually include a ground stake for use at the beach or at a campground. The grill and its charcoal pan adjust up and down and swing in or out; the grill can be used without the pan over a wood fire. Use charcoal briquettes with this grill indoors only in a well-ventilated fireplace since the charcoal produces carbon monoxide, which can be lethal in an enclosed space.

A large sheet of heavy wire netting cut to your specifications at the hardware store also makes a good grill. When it is placed over a fire, the flames are confined below the wire but it gets very hot for cooking.

No matter what you use for a grill, it is a good idea to coat it liberally with one of the natural vegetable spray-on coatings to keep foods from sticking and to make the potentially messy cleaning process much easier.

If you cook fish or meats over open fires you will probably want to invest in one of the following grills.

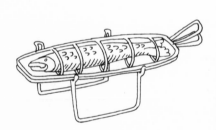

Fish Grill. This is an elongated wire "cradle" or basket designed to support the body of a fish over the coals without breaking it. The long handle allows you to cook one side of the fish, then flip the entire grill to cook the other side. The wires in this grill should be lightly greased before the fish is placed in it to avoid sticking. Fish grills are available in several sizes.

Grill Basket. This is an open container composed of two hinged wire trays which open to hold food between them for grilling. The basket has a long handle for easy manipulation over the coals. Use this utensil for grilling delicate foods which might break apart if placed alone on a grill. Fish and stuffed hamburgers should be cooked in this manner.

Hibachi. American picnickers have enthusiastically adopted a version of the Japanese hibachi, a small but heavy cast-iron grill fueled with charcoal heat. Temperatures can be regulated somewhat through the use of a small door or doors in the base of the grill. (The wider the door opening, the hotter the coals will be.) Hibachis are available in several sizes with adjustable wood-handled grills. A note of caution: Although the Japanese people traditionally use the hibachi indoors, our airtight modern methods of housing construction make it a dangerous practice because charcoal cooking creates toxic carbon monoxide. I have used the hibachi in a well-vented fireplace with several windows open when unexpected rain spoiled outdoor cooking plans. Better yet, use your hibachi on a screened porch when the rain washes out your picnic.

The popularity of hibachi-style cooking is growing due to its easy transport and to the growing number of areas restricting open fires. And it is much more economical to use than the many large electric and gas grills. Because of the hibachi's increased popularity, several styles are on the market, including one ingenious design enclosing the charcoal in a chimney-shaped portion which results in rapid heating of the charcoal. When the coals are hot, the chimney can be opened into two cooking surfaces with adjustable grills. When cooking is completed, the "chimney" can be closed to smother the fire. Ashes automatically sift into an ash drawer for easy disposal when cool, and unused charcoal can be retained for reuse. This model is particularly safe and very portable, making it a favorite with travellers who prefer to picnic alongside the road instead of eating in restaurants. For information on where to purchase the Hearth Craft Double Portable Barbecue, write to Hearth Craft, Inc., P.O. Box 13309, 7945 N.E. Alberta Street, Portland, Oregon 97213.

See page 32 for directions for starting charcoal-fueled fires.

Skewers. If you plan to do hibachi cooking or barbecuing on a grill, you will need skewers to spear chunks of meat, hot dogs, vegetables, marshmallows, even fruit. Skewers are available in stainless steel or bamboo. Look for metal skewers with wooden or plastic handles that make them easy and safe to hold over the heat of the fire. If you use bamboo skewers, be sure to soak them in water before using them to prevent their charring and/or burning.

Slow-Cooker. This small electric appliance uses low-watt, wraparound heating to cook foods over a long period of time. This method of preparation is said to enhance flavor and preserve the nutrients in the foods cooked. Since there is no heating from the bottom of the unit, tending the food is not necessary once it has been assembled in the crock of the slow-cooker. Typical cooking time for this appliance is 10 to 12 hours. It is available in several sizes and consists of an outer aluminum unit with an inner pottery crock which may or may not be removable. For picnic purposes (and versatility) those with removable crocks are best for carrying foods after home preparation. If you plan to cook picnic foods like Picnic Baked Beans (page 126), be sure to secure the lid of the pot during transport to maintain the interior temperature. It is also not a bad idea to wrap the crock in a thick layer of newspapers for additional insulation.

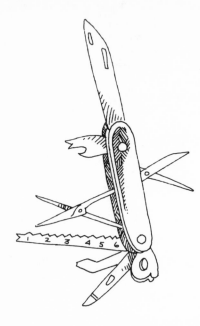

Swiss Army Knife. Most campers and backpackers find this all-purpose knife indispensable. It's a good addition to any picnic supply basket, and its versatility merits the relatively high price you will pay. It's designed to do everything from pull corks to spread mustard on hot dogs. The pocket model normally includes large and small pen knives, a nail file and manicure tool, scissors, screwdriver, tweezers and toothpick. Special models for fishing and hunting come with extra attachments including corkscrews and bottle openers.

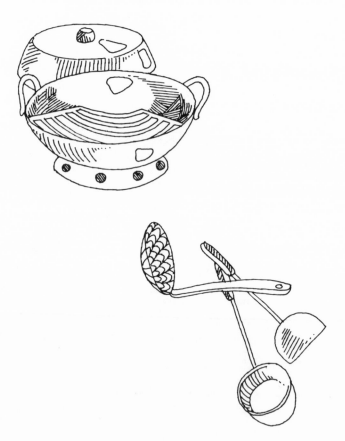

Wok. This versatile Oriental cooking pan is at home in many American kitchens but it also makes a good, all-purpose utensil for picnic cookouts. It is best when made of iron or steel. In this wide, curved-bottom pot you can poach, stir-fry, steam or simmer food—even boil water for coffee if necessary. Take along the metal collar to raise it above the high heat over which you will cook your picnic food.

Picnic First Aid

Since picnics often include outdoor activities—hiking, sports, games—injuries sometimes happen. Don't be caught unprepared. Make sure that a first-aid kit is automatically packed with your other picnic gear. Include the following items:

first-aid booklet

thermometer

adhesive tape

roll of gauze bandages

small scissors

4-inch-square sterile gauze pads

self-stick bandages in assorted sizes

sterile alcohol pads

mild soap and soft washcloth

antibiotic ointment for cuts and burns

tweezers and needles for removing splinters

matches

aspirin or aspirin substitute

antacid tablets for upset stomachs from too much picnic food

motion sickness pills

calamine lotion for poison ivy rash, prickly heat or bug bites

insect repellent

sunscreen and suntan lotion

ice bag for injured muscles or joints

Food and Fire Safety

Food is the star at a picnic, but it can sometimes play the villain and cause food poisoning. While fire plays a supporting role, its potential danger can be even greater. Keep picnic memories happy by observing the following rules for food preparation and fire use.

Food Safety

Salmonella, *Staphylococcus aureus*, *Clostridium perfringens* and *Clostridium botulinum* are not the names of exotic picnic foods. They are the bacteria that cause something picnickers dread: food poisoning. Unfortunately, these bacteria love some of the same foods that picnickers favor. To make it worse, contaminated foods often don't smell, taste or appear spoiled, so it's difficult to spot potential dangers.

Poor choice of picnic foods for hot weather, improper handling of foods during preparation and incorrect packing can lead to the several types of food poisoning with symptoms ranging from severe headaches and abdominal cramps to vomiting and diarrhea, or worse. Some types of food poisoning can cause death, especially in young children or older people. The best advice for preventing poisoning is to keep hot foods hot (140°F and above) and cold foods cold (45°F and below) to inhibit bacterial growth. In addition, heed the following precautions when selecting, preparing, packing and serving picnic foods.

■ Maintain good personal hygiene during food preparation and serving. Always wash hands thoroughly after handling raw meat, fish and poultry.

■ Thaw all meats and poultry in the refrigerator prior to preparation. Don't give bacteria a chance to grow by allowing meat to thaw on the kitchen counter.

■ Thoroughly wash all cutting utensils and cutting surfaces used for raw meat and poultry before using them for other food preparation.

■ Wash platters used for raw meat with soap and hot water before using them for prepared food.

■ After cooking, put foods, especially meats, moist dressings and custards, into the refrigerator immediately. Don't cool them on the counter.

■ Handle foods as little as possible before serving. If possible, make sandwiches at the picnic site. Pack the fixings on ice in separate containers.

■ If the picnic menu includes foods that contain mayonnaise, carry the mayonnaise in a jar or airtight plastic container on ice in the picnic cooler and mix it with the other ingredients just before serving. Examples include tuna fish and egg salads as well as an all-time picnic favorite, potato salad. If circumstances dictate home preparation of one of these salads, be sure to keep it well chilled up to the minute it's served—and after.

■ Keep serving dishes covered when dining outdoors. Flies are notorious disease carriers.

■ When packing the picnic cooler, don't overstock it. Air circulation allows the maintenance of lower temperatures and ensures optimum cooling. Pack mayonnaise, foods with uncooked or quick-cooked eggs or dairy products in them, and meats, fish and poultry closest to the ice. (When dry ice is used as the coolant, it should be packed on top of the food because the cooling gas, carbon dioxide, is heavier than air.) Keep these foods in the picnic cooler until you are ready to serve or cook them, and return them to the cooler after serving. Do not allow them to sit in the sun.

■ Thoroughly cook all meats with special attention paid to pork. A 1-inch-thick pork chop takes at least 20 minutes per side to cook until there is no pink color left in the meat. The internal temperature should be at least 170°F. If fried chicken is on the menu, keep it hot from the frying pan in a preheated insulated container (see page 17) or chill it thoroughly before packing it in the picnic cooler. Quickly cooked fried chicken held at lukewarm temperatures is a wonderful medium for bacterial growth.

■ Transfer hot casseroles to wide-mouthed thermal containers or wrap casseroles airtight in two layers of heavy-duty aluminum foil and then in several thicknesses of newspaper.

■ If you suspect food poisoning rather than a simple case of overeating to be the source of an after-picnic illness, contact everyone who ate the suspect food. Keep a sample of the food for the local health inspector to test.

Don't become a food poisoning statistic! This dread malady is particularly prevalent from May to October when warm weather supports the growth of food-poisoning bacteria, so pay particular attention to preparing and packing your picnic meals. Be especially careful with foods high in protein and those containing eggs and dairy products.

What About Wild Foods?

Due to ever-encroaching suburbia, one of the disappearing delights of outdoor eating—especially for backpackers and hikers—is the use of wild foods to supplement picnic foods. Wild berries and mushrooms as well as mint, watercress, asparagus, fiddlehead ferns and day lily sprouts are just a few of the many wild foods that can add distinctive flavors to your picnic meal. But a word of caution is in order: KNOW WHAT YOU EAT! Don't eat anything that you cannot positively identify as safely edible. There are several good books available on the subject of wild foods. Check with your local librarian or wilderness survival club for more information on learning to identify and enjoy wild foods, free for the finding.

Fire Safety

If your picnic plans include outdoor cooking, whether over campfire, stove or hibachi, extreme caution is recommended. If you use a stove (see page 23 for general descriptions of available types), be sure that you have read the accompanying directions thoroughly before igniting the fuel source. It's a good idea to pack the instruction sheet with the stove as a matter of course. Protect the instructions by encasing them front and back with a clear adhesive-backed vinyl covering. Tape them to the inside lid of your picnic basket for safekeeping. Most importantly, be sure to use the correct fuel for the stove you've chosen. The wrong fuel in a stove can cause an explosion that could leave you without fingers, an arm, even your life! Above all, never leave any fire, in a stove or otherwise contained, untended—not even for a second.

Charcoal Fire-Building

No matter what cooking receptacle you use for a charcoal fire, the method of building and testing the fire is relatively simple. Build charcoal fires outdoors, or in rain emergencies on a well-ventilated porch or in a well-vented fireplace with windows open for extra air circulation. Charcoal fires produce carbon monoxide which is lethal in an unventilated area!

Charcoal fires take time to prepare since foods are normally cooked over hot coals, not over a blazing fire. Plan to start the coals, commercially available in briquette form, at least 30 to 45 minutes before cooking time. Adhere to the following steps to ensure the best fire for cooking purposes.

1. If your hibachi or barbecue grill does not have a removable ash pan, first line the bottom with heavy-duty foil, shiny side up, to make cleanup easy. The foil also acts as a heat reflector.

2. Heap charcoal briquettes in the center of the hibachi or grill. Don't use too many. When hot, the coals should just cover the bottom of the grill in a single layer. Set them aflame with a long fireplace match. Charcoal can be difficult to start. If so, a commercial charcoal starter or lighter fluid can be lightly sprinkled on the briquettes *before* ignition. NEVER SQUIRT STARTER FLUID ON A WORKING FIRE! Large flareups are the result, often causing unnecessary injury. Some people feel that starter fluids give an off-taste to foods, but you might not agree. Even if you do, a little off-taste is better than no fire at all, entirely possible with finicky charcoal. Just use the starter sparingly or use a solid or semisolid fire starter (see page 25). NEVER USE KEROSENE OR GASOLINE TO START A FIRE! They're extremely dangerous.

3. Allow the ignited coals to burn until they are covered with a white or gray ash, then use long-handled tongs to separate the hot coals into an even layer under the space you plan to use for grilling the food. Arrange them polka-dot fashion for grilling meats and solid foods, and in rows between skewers of food.

4. To test the fire for cooking heat, hold your bare hand over the prepared charcoal fire at the same level you plan to cook the food and count using the "one thousand one, one thousand two," method. Use the number of seconds you can hold your hand comfortably over the fire to gauge the heat. If you can keep your hand there only one or two seconds, the fire is relatively *hot* and suitable for grilling steaks, kabobs and hamburgers. Three- and four-second fires are *medium*, best for roasts and large pieces of meat. Five- and six-second fires are relatively *slow*, good for keeping foods warm and toasting marshmallows on green sticks or skewers.

5. To increase heat in a charcoal fire, lower the food grill, open the drafts wider, move the coals closer together and, if necessary, add more hot briquettes which can be started in an old cake pan if you anticipate the need for more. Use long-handled tongs to add hot coals. The reverse of these steps will reduce the heat if necessary. If all else fails to lower the heat, remove some of the coals or sprinkle them with a little water.

6. When cooking is completed, close the draft and allow the coals to cool. Discard the ashes only when they are cold, and retain half-used briquettes to start future fires.

Hints for Charcoal Cooking
■ To give charcoal-cooked meats subtle flavor, sprinkle the hot coals with fresh herbs like thyme, mint or basil, or use dried herbs like bay leaves, tarragon or fennel soaked in a little water.

■ To prevent steaks and chops from curling on the grill, remove large pieces of excess fat and score the edges of the meat.

■ To seal in meat juices, first quickly sear the meat on both sides by lowering the grill close to the hot fire. Then move the grill away from the coals and use tongs to turn the meat. Be careful to avoid puncturing the meat which would allow the juices to seep out, drying out the meat and causing the flames to flare up.

■ If you are grilling foods with a marinade high in sugar content, you can anticipate periodic flame flareups. Therefore, never leave the fire untended and keep a plastic sprinkler or spray bottle handy to douse the flames. Sugary marinades should be used for basting only during the last 15 minutes of cooking.

■ Brush charcoal grills with vegetable oil or spray them with a vegetable coating to make cleanup easy. Clean grills as soon as they are cool enough to safely touch. Caked-on grease and food remnants will adversely affect foods cooked at another time.

Foil-Wrapped Food Packets for Outdoor Cooking

To seal in tasty cooking juices and prevent unnecessary dripping, foods to be cooked over a campfire, on a grill or in the coals can be carefully wrapped in heavy-duty aluminum foil. The best wrapping method is commonly referred to as the "drugstore wrap."

1. Place food in the center of the shiny side of a piece of heavy-duty foil a little larger than the food to be wrapped.

2. Bring two opposite edges of the foil together and fold them in an interlocking seam as shown.

3. After making the seam, continue folding the seam down to the food to enclose it snugly but leaving a little room for steam expansion during cooking.

4. Turn the packet carefully so that the seam is against the table.

5. Fold the unsealed ends as shown, being sure to force excess air from the packet before sealing the last end.

NOTE: If packets contain runny liquids, it may not be possible to do Step 4. In that case, complete Step 5 without turning the packet.

Building a Campfire

If you plan to build a fire to cook outdoors, the first rule is to be sure you check the laws regarding fire building in the area. Open fires are being restricted more and more, so check with city officials, forest rangers or camp proprietors for necessary permits. You might need such a permit, even if you plan to build a charcoal fire in your hibachi. During dry spells, outdoor fires are sometimes banned on short notice. Before you light the match be sure you're not breaking a law.

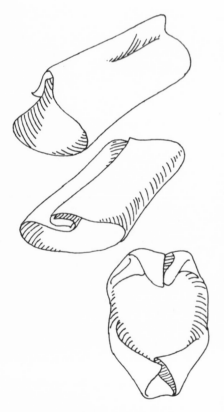

Location. Choose the location for your fire with great care. Look for a rocky spot, a sandy stretch of ground, or soil with high mineral content. Avoid loamy ground with high organic content which burns readily. Be sure the spot you choose has no overhanging branches lower than 10 feet. Deadwood still attached to a tree should be even higher away from the fire site. If you build your fire in an exposed place, you run the risk of increased danger from flying sparks should a wind come up. Wind will also cause your fire to heat poorly and you will need to use a lot more wood.

Materials. The most successful fires are carefully laid using three materials—tinder, kindling and firewood—surrounded by rocks for balancing grills and/or pans. Choose rocks of similar size and shape, each with at least one relatively flat surface. Do not use rocks from a stream bed as the water they contain will turn to steam which could cause the rocks to explode—and your dinner along with them!

Tinder is the fire starter and may be anything from dry moss to a vacated mouse or bird nest. Match-size sticks and twigs, crumpled paper or waxed paper can be used, too. Natural tinder sources include dry birch bark torn into strips and loosely wadded, dry cedar bark and dry grass or weeds crushed in a loose wad. Even slivers of pitch will do the trick.

Kindling is set upright over the wadded tinder in the fireplace, teepee fashion. Use thin, dry, pencil-size sticks of wood no larger than ½ inch thick. See page 25 for directions on how to gather and prepare small bundles of kindling for use as fire starters. Be sure to leave some airspace between the tinder and the kindling for the flow of oxygen to feed the fire.

Firewood comes in several varieties but you will be limited to what is dry and readily available in the picnic area; or you can borrow a few logs from your home fireplace supply if you have the room and inclination to carry them along. The best wood for campfires is hardwood—ash, oak, birch and maple. The fires from these woods will be hotter, last longer and result in a better bed of coals. In some areas you might be limited to the wood from evergreen trees—pine, spruce and fir. Because of their high resin content, evergreens burn with a lot of snapping and popping—and more sparks. Meats roasted over open fires using these woods sometimes acquire a sharp, resiny taste, so it's best to let such fires burn down until they're almost reduced to coals to avoid the off-flavor. Split logs and deadwood branches should be at least 4 inches thick for a strong, steady fire.

Use the following procedure to build the best cooking fires.

1. Choose a safe location, as outlined above, about 6 feet in diameter.

2. Clear the area of debris.

3. Select large rocks and work them down into the earth with the flattest surfaces exposed. Arrange them in a U shape with the open end pointing into the wind to facilitate feeding the fire; or use the keyhole shape with a 6- to 8-inch-wide slit pointing toward the wind.

4. Place tinder in the center of the fireplace, then arrange kindling, teepee fashion, above it.

5. Finally, arrange firewood over the kindling, also teepee fashion. Be sure to leave airspace for oxygen flow between the kindling and the firewood.

6. Light the fire by touching a long fireplace match to the tinder on the upwind side, and coax it with fanning and blowing.

7. If using the keyhole-style fireplace, as the coals form, push them to the slit of the keyhole for a cooking area with even, constant heat. Prop pans on the rocks or place a portable grill (see page 25) on the rocks over the hot coals to hold your cooking utensils.

8. To quench the fire, stir the ashes and pour water on everything. Dip still-burning logs in water. Stir the firebed until the last wisp of steam disappears, and don't leave the area until you know that you could touch the firebed with your bare hands without fear of burns.

9. NEVER LEAVE A FIRE UNTENDED, even for just a few seconds. Flying sparks, gone unnoticed, could be the end of your favorite picnic spot.

THE PICNIC MENUS

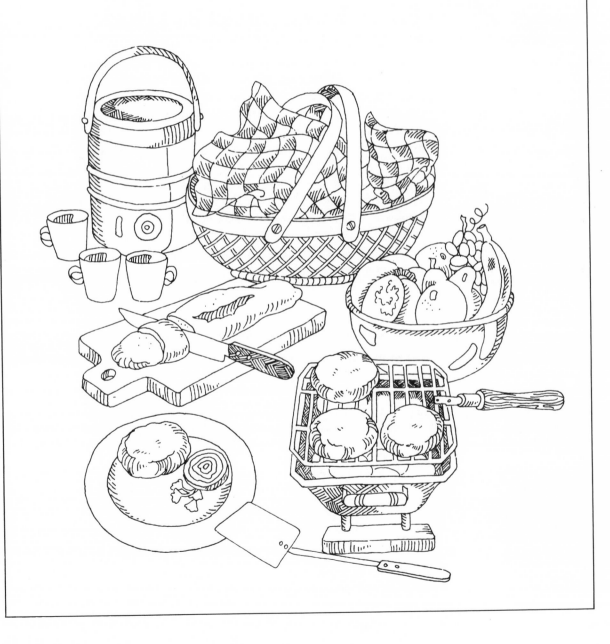

Spring Excursions
Dining Amid Flowers

Bikers' Easy Gourmet Backpack

Not only is this picnic especially suited to bikers' backpacks, it's easy to prepare as well. For that reason, it's dedicated to a good friend who lobbied for "easy picnics for Susy" while I was writing this book! In fact, the main course is based on one of her favorite quick recipes. It's best to prepare everything the night before you plan to pedal off for the lush spring meadows and fresh-scented woods. At takeoff time, divide the goodies between backpacks so no one has to bear the entire load. Carry the dressing for Vegetable Confetti in a thermal container and to make sure the Liebfraumilch or juice is icy cold, buy it in individual-size bottles, then pack each in ice-filled plastic bags (doubled or tripled to prevent leaks). Surround each bag with a terry washcloth or small dish towel to absorb any leaks. Of course, you can always plan to look for a picnic spot beside a cold stream where you can chill the wine!

COLD SHRIMP VINAIGRETTE

30 to 36 jumbo shrimp, still in their shells
½ cup water
1½ cups olive oil
⅔ cup red wine vinegar
5 cloves garlic, minced (more or less, to your liking)
2 cups finely chopped fresh parsley
pinch of salt

1. Place all ingredients except 1 cup of the parsley in a wide, shallow saucepan over medium heat and cook until shrimp are done, about 3 to 4 minutes. Do not allow shrimp to curl. Remove from heat. Chill shrimp in the cooking juices.

2. To serve, transfer the shrimp to a serving platter and sprinkle with the remaining parsley.

Serves 6

PICNIC NOTE: Allow 6 shrimp per person to serve this dish as an entrée, fewer for appetizers.

SUSY'S EASY HERB JAR CHICKEN

This recipe is particularly easy and takes no more than an hour to prepare, start to finish. The recipe is from a friend who rarely plans ahead and she says it tastes great warm from the oven. But if you do plan ahead, it gets better if it is allowed to develop its flavors for a day in the refrigerator. It can taste very different each time you prepare it, based on what is available in your herb jars. Just be sure that when mixed, you have about 1 tablespoon of mixed herbs for each chicken breast. *Note:* This recipe is for purchased dried herbs, not for fresh ones.

6 whole chicken breasts, split and skinned, and boned if desired	3 tablespoons dried chervil
	salt and pepper to taste
1 clove garlic, peeled	2 tablespoons finely chopped onion
3 tablespoons dried tarragon	3 to 6 tablespoons olive oil
3 tablespoons parsley flakes	Parmesan cheese (optional)
3 tablespoons chopped chives	

1. Preheat oven to 375° F.

2. Wash chicken breasts and pat dry. Rub each breast on both sides with garlic.

3. Mix herbs and chopped onion together in a small bowl.

4. Place a few tablespoons of oil in a shallow pan. Dip chicken breasts in oil to lightly coat, then roll in herb mixture and place in a very lightly oiled baking pan.

5. Sprinkle breasts with any remaining herbs and Parmesan cheese (if desired). Bake for 15 minutes. Reduce heat to 350° F and bake an additional 30 to 40 minutes.

6. Serve warm or cold.

Serves 6 to 12

Variations: Rosemary, oregano, thyme, basil, paprika, even sesame seeds can be substituted or added to the herb mixture given for a change in taste each time you use this recipe. Firm white fish or boiled, peeled shrimp can be substituted for the chicken. Just dip the fish in a little melted butter or margarine instead of oil, then roll in herbs and bake at 350°F for 30 to 40 minutes. Serve warm or cold with fresh lemon wedges.

PICNIC NOTE: If you plan to serve the chicken warm, transfer it immediately from the baking pan to a wide-mouthed thermal container. If you're serving it cold, carry to the picnic in a cooler.

VEGETABLE CONFETTI

1½ pounds red potatoes
5 tablespoons olive oil
1 medium-size onion, chopped
½ pound fresh mushrooms, sliced
1 tablespoon dried basil
⅛ to ¼ teaspoon cayenne pepper
1 teaspoon dry mustard
1 teaspoon salt
1 teaspoon sugar
3 tablespoons lemon juice
2 carrots, coarsely grated
2 stalks celery, sliced
½ cup chopped fresh parsley
½ cup chopped kosher dill pickle
½ cup plain yogurt
½ cup dairy sour cream
10 slices crisply fried bacon, drained and crumbled

1. Scrub potatoes and cook in their jackets in salted water until fork-tender. Drain, cool, peel and dice, and place in a large bowl.

2. Heat oil in a heavy skillet over medium-high heat. Add onion, mushrooms and basil, and cook until onion is limp and transparent and juice has evaporated. Remove from heat and stir in cayenne, mustard, salt, sugar and lemon juice. Lift from pan with a slotted spoon and place in bowl with diced potatoes.

3. Add carrots, celery, parsley and pickle, and toss gently to blend. Refrigerate, covered, 4 hours or overnight.

4. Just before serving, stir in the yogurt, the sour cream and the crumbled bacon.

Serves 6 to 8

PICNIC NOTE: Take the chilled vegetables, the yogurt and sour cream and the crumbled bacon to the picnic in three separate containers and mix prior to serving.

BRANDIED TOMATOES

This salad is so easy and very tasty. Use only vine-ripened, smooth-skinned tomatoes, and allow picnickers to dress the marinated tomatoes to their liking.

6 large ripe tomatoes	walnut or peanut oil
salt and pepper to taste	finely chopped fresh parsley
2 to 3 tablespoons brandy vinegar	finely chopped fresh basil

1. Cut tomatoes into wedges and place them in a shallow dish.

2. Sprinkle with salt and pepper to taste and sprinkle liberally with brandy. Allow them to marinate at room temperature at least 1 hour.

3. Drain and serve with a dash of vinegar and oil, and sprinkle with finely chopped parsley and/or basil.

Serves 6

EASY CARAMEL CUSTARD

This easy recipe is probably very old. Two friends from different parts of the country both shared it with me because they thought it would be an easy dessert to pack in a picnic basket. The lengthy cooking time causes the sugar content of the milk to caramelize in the can.

one 14-ounce can sweetened condensed milk	one 8-ounce can sliced pineapple (four slices)

1. Remove and discard paper label from the can of condensed milk. Place can of milk in a small saucepan and cover with water.

2. Bring to a boil, then lower heat and simmer 2½ to 3 hours, adding water as necessary to keep the can covered. To avoid pressure build-up and possible explosion, DO NOT COVER THE PAN. Remove can from the water with tongs and cool.

3. To serve, open both ends of the can and slide the custard out. Slice into 4 servings and place each slice of custard on top of a slice of pineapple.

Serves 4

PICNIC NOTE: Don't forget the can opener!

Child's Hobo Lunch

MENU

Milk

**Celery Ribs with Peanut
Butter Spread***

Montana Miners' Pasties*

Apple Wheels*

Honey Bran Cookies*

Wrap up this lunch in big bandannas and tie them to old broom handles or dowels for the kids to carry over their shoulders hobo-style to a nearby park on a warm spring day. The novelty of the idea will surely appeal to almost any child, and the foods inside the bandannas, which serve as individual tablecloths, won't go uneaten—crunchy celery ribs filled with a sweet peanut butter spread, pastries filled with meat and potatoes, followed by apples filled with chocolate and Honey Bran Cookies for dessert. All the foods will travel well in a bandanna and, unless the hike is a long one, only the milk requires refrigeration to keep it icy cold. Just put it in small individual thermoses in each bandanna or let one child be responsible for carrying it in a larger thermos.

Why not try this picnic for a unique birthday party? Just substitute a cake for the dessert—try Sour Cream Fudge Cake (page 211), or Chocolate Cream Cheese Pound Cake (page 186)—and don't forget the candles.

PEANUT BUTTER SPREAD

This recipe happened by accident but you won't believe how good it is until you try it!

4 tablespoons butter	1 cup peanut butter,
1 cup finely chopped onion	crunchy or smooth
4 tablespoons sugar	

1. In a small saucepan, melt butter and sauté onion.

2. Stir in the sugar, mix well and bring to a boil. Reduce heat and stir in the peanut butter. Mix well and stir constantly, cooking until peanut butter is melted and heated through. Remove from heat and cool. Store in refrigerator.

3. Use as filling for celery ribs; also delicious on sandwiches.

Yield: 1¼ cups spread

MONTANA MINERS' PASTIES

A friend who grew up in the mining town of Butte, Montana, remembers these meat-and-vegetable-filled pasties as favorite childhood picnic fare. Welsh miners in Butte carried them in their lunch boxes because they are tasty and filling, and travel well.

1 recipe Rich Pastry (page 189)
1 pound sirloin, cut into ¼- to ½-inch cubes
1 large raw potato, washed, peeled and finely chopped
1 small onion, finely chopped
2 scallions, finely chopped (including part of the green tops)

2 to 3 large carrots, finely chopped
1 tablespoon parsley flakes
salt and pepper to taste
dash of garlic powder (optional)
butter
1 egg yolk
1 tablespoon cream or milk

1. Preheat oven to 375°F.

2. Prepare pastry and set aside.

3. Combine the meat, vegetables and seasonings, and toss to mix well.

4. Divide prepared pastry into 10 to 12 small balls. On a lightly floured surface, roll each pastry ball out to ⅛-inch-thick circles about 5 to 6 inches in diameter.

5. Spoon about ¼ to ⅓ cup of the meat mixture onto one half of each pastry circle. Dot with butter. Moisten edge of circle with a little water, then fold in half and press edges together with the tines of a fork. Make a slash in the top of each pastry to allow cooking steam to escape.

6. Beat egg yolk with cream and brush over each pasty. Place pasties on an ungreased baking sheet and bake for 45 minutes to 1 hour. Pasties should be golden brown. Cool on a cake rack.

7. Serve hot or cold with ketchup if you wish.

Yield: 10 to 12 pasties (serves 5 to 6 as an entrée)

APPLE WHEELS

6 medium-size apples, cored
four 1-ounce squares
    semisweet chocolate

4 teaspoons creamy peanut
    butter
4 tablespoons honey
¼ cup finely chopped peanuts

1. Enlarge the center of each cored apple to about 1 inch. Cover the bottom of each apple with aluminum foil to seal.

2. Combine chocolate and peanut butter in a small saucepan and partially melt over very low heat. Remove from heat and stir rapidly until completely melted.

3. Stir in honey and peanuts and blend well. Quickly spoon mixture into the apples. Chill until chocolate is firm, about 45 minutes.

4. Remove foil from the apples, then slice apples crosswise. (If apples are chilled longer than 1 hour before slicing, let them stand at room temperature for at least 5 minutes before slicing.) Serve immediately.

Serves 6

PICNIC NOTE: To prevent discoloration of the apples, do not slice them until you're ready to serve them. The apples can also be eaten whole.

HONEY BRAN COOKIES

¾ cup all-purpose flour
3 cups all-bran cereal (not
    bran flakes)
½ cup sugar
¼ teaspoon cinnamon
¼ teaspoon ground ginger

½ teaspoon baking soda
½ cup honey
½ cup milk
½ cup butter or margarine,
    melted

1. Preheat oven to 375°F.

2. Combine dry ingredients.

3. Mix honey, milk and butter together. Stir into dry ingredients and mix thoroughly.

4. Drop by teaspoonfuls onto a greased baking sheet or into midget-size foil baking cups, and bake for 12 to 15 minutes, until cookies are golden.

Yield: 5 to 6 dozen cookies

Japanese Celebration of Spring

Celebrate the arrival of spring with a family outing to a local park or botanical garden to soak up the fresh scents of the new foliage and to enjoy a Japanese picnic lunch. The Japanese are said to be in constant quest for harmony with nature, so it seems obvious that they would incorporate picnics into their well-ordered lives on a regular basis. In fact, they are such great picnic fanciers that they have designed beautiful compartmentalized containers to carry picnic foods. These age-old "bento boxes" are filled with picnic foods for family outings, workday lunches, travel meals, and snacks for intermission at the theater. This springtime picnic menu includes a traditional picnic food, sushi, as well as other tasty Japanese foods. Both Japanese ingredients and American substitutes are noted wherever possible. Don't hesitate to make the substitutions if you cannot locate the traditional ingredients at an Oriental or gourmet food store.

MENU

Sake on Ice*   Iced Green Tea

Nori-Maki Sushi*
with Dipping Sauce*

Pickled Ginger

Sweet-Sour Asparagus
with Walnuts*

Shrimp in Lemon Cups*

Fresh Fruit

Plum Wine

SAKE ON ICE

For each serving:
3 ounces sake
crushed ice

green tea (brewed with tea leaves, then cooled)
lime slice

1. Pour sake over ice, then fill the glass with cooled green tea.

2. Garnish with a slice of lime.

PICNIC NOTE: Carry crushed ice in a small thermal container and cooled green tea in another. Mix each drink at the picnic. Serve plain, iced green tea as an alternative or take along chilled carbonated beverages.

NORI-MAKI SUSHI

Sushi is the term used to describe a wide variety of cold Japanese snacks, each made with a base of vinegared rice. Each sushi, no matter the kind, is meant to be a single mouthful. A favorite Japanese picnic food carried in bento boxes, sushi is particularly adaptable to American picnics as a main course, hors d'oeuvre or appetizer. Preparation is time-consuming until you've had a little practice but the results are well worth the effort. A variety of sushi can also be purchased from a Japanese restaurant for take-out, if you prefer to leave preparation to the experts.

1 whole chicken breast	1 small zucchini
1 stalk celery, sliced	8 to 10 sheets laver seaweed (nori)
¼ cup Mirin (rice wine) or pale dry sherry	1 recipe Sushi Rice (page 47)
¼ teaspoon salt	1 tablespoon wasabi powder (Japanese horseradish) mixed to a paste with 1 tablespoon water (or substitute 1 tablespoon prepared horseradish)
3 to 4 dried Japanese mushrooms	
½ cup chicken broth, strained	
3 tablespoons Japanese soy sauce	
1 tablespoon sugar	
1 tablespoon Mirin or pale dry sherry	8 to 10 sprigs Italian parsley
1 small cucumber, peeled and seeded	Dipping Sauce (page 48) pickled red ginger

1. Wipe chicken breast with damp cloth and place it in a small saucepan with celery, ¼ cup Mirin, salt and water to cover. Bring to a boil, then simmer 45 minutes. Remove from broth and cool. Set broth aside for later use.

2. While chicken cooks, soak mushrooms in cold water for 20 minutes or until soft. Drain and slice into long, thin strips.

3. Combine ½ cup strained reserved chicken broth, the soy sauce, sugar and 1 tablespoon Mirin in a small saucepan. Add mushrooms and cook until liquid is almost absorbed and mushrooms are well flavored. Drain and reserve mushrooms.

4. Cut cucumber and zucchini into sticks about ¼ inch in diameter and 3 to 4 inches long.

5. Remove skin from cooled chicken and cut chicken into strips about the same size as the cucumber and zucchini.

6. Toast one side of each sheet of the seaweed by holding with tongs over a flame for a few moments until crisp. Toast eight sheets of the seaweed before proceeding to next step.

7. Place one sheet of seaweed on a bamboo mat or heavy cloth napkin. Spread approximately 1 cup of Sushi Rice evenly over the bottom two-thirds of the sheet.

8. Across the center of the rice, place a strip of mushroom, chicken dabbed with a little wasabi, a stick of cucumber or zucchini and a sprig of parsley.

9. Roll the sushi tightly in the bamboo mat or napkin, pressing firmly so that the ingredients adhere to each other in a neat cylinder.

10. Remove the bamboo mat or napkin and, with a sharp knife, cut the rolled sushi into eight equal slices. For best results in cutting, first pull the knife toward you as you cut halfway through the roll, then push down and away from yourself to cut through the remainder. Wipe the knife with a damp cloth after each cut.

11. Repeat the process described above until all the rice and vegetables are used.

12. Arrange sushi cylinders in an attractive pattern in a serving platter and serve with small saucers of Dipping Sauce and slices of pickled red ginger to eat after each piece of sushi.

Yield: 64 to 80 pieces (serves 6 to 8 as an entrée)

SUSHI RICE

3 cups raw Japanese or unconverted white rice
3¾ cups water
one 5-inch piece of kelp (kombu)
3 tablespoons Mirin (rice wine) or pale dry sherry
⅓ cup rice vinegar or mild white vinegar
2 tablespoons sugar
1 teaspoon monosodium glutamate (optional)

1. Wash rice thoroughly and allow to drain for 1 hour.

2. Put rice, water and kelp in a heavy saucepan and allow to soak 30 minutes. Remove kelp.

3. Add Mirin to rice and bring to a boil. Reduce heat, cover and simmer rice 15 to 20 minutes or until it is just tender. Remove from heat and allow to stand, covered, for about 10 minutes.

4. Combine vinegar, sugar and monosodium glutamate (if desired) in a small saucepan over low heat, and heat through.

5. Transfer rice to a large wooden bowl or enamel pan. Quickly add heated vinegar mixture to the rice and, using a spatula, make cutting motions through the rice to ensure even distribution of the seasonings.

6. Cool the rice by fanning by hand or with an electric fan and stirring constantly until it is cool. This makes the rice shiny and prevents it from becoming mushy.

Yield: about 9 cups

DIPPING SAUCE

1   cup chicken broth
½   cup sugar
½   cup Japanese soy sauce
2   tablespoons Mirin (rice wine) or sherry

2   teaspoons grated fresh ginger (optional)

1. Combine all ingredients in a shaker jar and shake vigorously to blend.

2. Serve at room temperature in individual dipping bowls.

Yield: about 1¾ cups

SWEET-SOUR ASPARAGUS WITH WALNUTS

2   pounds fresh young asparagus, or two 10-ounce packages frozen asparagus spears
20 whole, shelled walnuts
10 tablespoons sugar

6   tablespoons Japanese soy sauce
6   tablespoons rice vinegar or distilled cider vinegar
pepper to taste

1. Cook asparagus in boiling, lightly salted water, uncovered, until just tender, about 8 to 10 minutes. Drain.

2. Crush walnuts and combine with remaining ingredients to make the dressing.

3. Pour dressing over asparagus and toss gently. Sprinkle with pepper to taste.

Serves 6

SHRIMP IN LEMON CUPS

6 large lemons	3 tablespoons grated radish
one 10¼-ounce can tiny shrimp, drained (reserve the most attractive for garnish, if desired)	2 tablespoons rice vinegar or distilled cider vinegar
	1 teaspoon sugar
	1 teaspoon Japanese soy sauce
1 medium-size cucumber, peeled and finely diced	1 teaspoon grated fresh ginger
	salt to taste
3 scallions, finely sliced (including part of the green tops)	cucumber slices (optional)
	scallion greens (optional)
	radish slices (optional)

1. Soak lemons in very hot tap water for 5 minutes, then roll firmly between your palm and the counter top to loosen inner pulp.

2. Cut a thick slice from one end of each lemon. Carefully squeeze juice from the large portion of the lemon into a small bowl and reserve. Carefully remove pulp and membrane from each lemon and discard. If necessary, cut a thin slice from the other end of each lemon so that it will stand upright.

3. Combine shrimp with remaining ingredients and enough of the reserved lemon juice to moisten. Toss well.

4. If desired, serve lemon shells stuffed with mixture and topped with additional shrimp, cucumber slices cut in wedges, pieces of scallion green cut on the diagonal and slices of radish. Or simply pack mixture into lemon shells and cover with their "lids."

Serves 6

PICNIC NOTE: Pack lemons upright and close together in a small airtight container to transport to the picnic site. Keep chilled.

Fresh Catch (or Catch as Catch Can)

Nothing tastes better than fish straight from the stream to your frying pan. Unless the fish always swallow your bait, though, don't count on being able to feed all your hungry picnickers through your fishing efforts alone. Pack a hearty lunch that will complement a fresh catch if you're lucky or fill a tummy even if it was not the day for reeling them in. If you're all set for the taste of fish over a campfire, pack fresh or frozen fish on ice in the picnic cooler just in case a "live one" doesn't make it to your hot coals or you need to supplement the catch of the day. Whether it's fresh or frozen, be sure to pack a grill basket (page 26) for cooking. Keep the standby fish frozen until you know whether you'll need it. If it's your lucky day and you catch enough to feed the crowd, take the standby home and use it within a few days.

This menu takes advantage of the cooking fire you'll need for the fish. You can use it to cook the packets of mushrooms and peas. Even the potatoes can be cooked over the campfire, or they can be prepared ahead and kept warm in a thermal container. Fresh Apple Cake, if you have room, is a great finale. It's delicious! Be sure to pack plenty of nibbles—fresh fruit, nuts, crackers—for the anglers to munch on while they reel in the catch.

TEA PUNCH

1 cup very strong tea
1 quart boiling water
2 cups sugar
one 6-ounce can frozen lemonade concentrate
1 cup orange juice
one 8-ounce can crushed pineapple (including canning syrup)
1 quart lemon-lime soda or 1 bottle white wine

1. Combine tea, boiling water and sugar in a gallon thermal container. Allow to cool.

2. Add lemonade concentrate, orange juice and crushed pineapple. Chill.

3. To serve, strain to remove pineapple if desired. Dilute with soda or wine.

Yield: 2½ to 3 quarts

GREEN AND WHITE SALAD

2 large ripe avocados,
    peeled, halved, pitted
    and sliced
lemon juice
2 white grapefruit, peeled
    and thinly sliced
    crosswise
4 ripe kiwi fruit, peeled and
    sliced crosswise

2 large stalks celery, sliced
Creamy Pear Dressing to
    moisten (page 173)
1 cup alfalfa sprouts
    (page 195)
Boston lettuce

1. Sprinkle avocado slices liberally with lemon juice to prevent discoloration.

2. Combine avocado with grapefruit, kiwi fruit slices and celery. Top with Creamy Pear Dressing to moisten. Toss gently.

3. Just prior to serving, sprinkle salad with alfalfa sprouts. Serve in leaves of Boston lettuce.

Serves 6

Variation: If you enjoy the combination of onions with fruit, add several sliced scallions before tossing with the dressing.

FRESH CATCH

Try any one of the following methods for preparing the catch of the day (gutted and cleaned).

1. Rub the fish with salt, pepper and basil, and wrap it in strips of bacon or coat it lightly with cooking oil. Cook in grill basket over gray coals for 5 to 10 minutes per side, depending on the thickness of the fish.

2. Place a mixture of chopped onion, celery and your favorite herb(s)—basil, dill, tarragon or fennel—in the cavity. Brush the outside lightly with cooking oil. Slash body of fish diagonally to prevent curling. Cook in a grill basket as directed above.

3. Lightly coat outsides of small whole fish with oil, then roll in cornmeal. Pan fry in a little butter or bacon fat.

4. Prepare as directed for Grilled Fish Steaks (page 52).

GRILLED FISH STEAKS

½ cup lemon juice
½ cup olive oil
3 tablespoons finely
　chopped fresh parsley
½ teaspoon salt

dash of pepper
six ½-pound salmon or
　halibut steaks
2 bunches scallions

1. Mix lemon juice, oil, parsley, salt and pepper together in bowl.

2. Brush fish steaks generously with marinade. Allow to stand at least 30 minutes.

3. Clean scallions, leaving all of the green tops intact.

4. Arrange scallions in a row on the grill, positioned 5 to 6 inches above glowing coals. Place marinated fish steaks on top of scallions. Cook over coals for about 25 to 30 minutes, turning once. Baste often with marinade while cooking.

5. To serve, lift steaks from the bed of scallions with a wide spatula. Discard scallions.

Serves 6

SHERRIED MUSHROOMS WITH PEAS

½ pound fresh mushrooms
2 to 4 tablespoons butter or
　margarine
3 tablespoons sherry
salt and pepper to taste

½ teaspoon cinnamon
¼ teaspoon nutmeg
two 10-ounce packages
　frozen peas

1. Wipe mushrooms with a damp cloth and trim stems. Slice.

2. Melt butter in a heavy saucepan. Add mushrooms and sauté. When almost done, add sherry, salt and pepper to taste, cinnamon and nutmeg. Bring to a boil and simmer for 1 minute. Turn off heat and let stand.

3. Place each block of frozen peas on a large square of heavy-duty aluminum foil. Spoon sherried mushrooms and the cooking liquid over the peas.

4. Seal each package as illustrated on page 34.

5. Place packages on a grill over hot coals for 10 to 15 minutes, turning occasionally.

Serves 6 to 8

PICNIC NOTE: Pack prepared packets in a covered leakproof container to carry to the picnic.

LEMON POTATOES PIQUANT

It's hard to believe how good these are!

2 pounds red potatoes (about 6 to 8 medium-size)	½ cup sugar
	1 tablespoon lemon juice
	1 teaspoon dried basil
½ cup butter or margarine	grated lemon rind

1. Peel potatoes and slice thickly. Parboil in lightly salted water for 5 to 10 minutes. They should still be slightly crisp. Drain.

2. While potatoes are cooking, combine butter, sugar, lemon juice and basil in a large heavy skillet. Heat slowly, stirring constantly, until butter is melted and resulting syrup is bubbly.

3. Add drained potatoes to syrup and cook over low heat for 10 to 15 minutes, until the potatoes are richly glazed. Spoon syrup over potatoes often during cooking period.

4. To serve, sprinkle with lemon rind.

Variations: I can't think of a single fresh vegetable that wouldn't taste elegant cooked in a similar fashion. Try carrots, green beans, peas, asparagus, sweet potatoes, beets or broccoli.

FRESH APPLE CAKE

3 cups sifted all-purpose flour	2 eggs, lightly beaten
2 cups sugar	¾ cup vegetable oil
1 teaspoon baking powder	1 teaspoon vanilla
1 teaspoon baking soda	3 cups chopped apples (with skins)
½ teaspoon salt	
1 teaspoon cinnamon	1 cup raisins
½ teaspoon ground cloves	1 cup finely chopped walnuts

1. Preheat oven to 350°F.

2. Measure sifted flour into a large mixing bowl. Add sugar, baking powder and soda, salt and spices, and mix well.

3. Stir in eggs, oil and vanilla. Mixture will be crumbly.

4. Add apples, raisins and walnuts, and mix well.

5. Spoon mixture into a well-greased 10-inch tube pan and bake for 1 hour and 10 minutes or until toothpick inserted in center comes out clean. Remove from tube pan to wire rack and cool.

Serves 12

PICNIC NOTE: Wrap whole or in slices in aluminum foil or transparent wrap to transport to picnic site.

May Day Picnic Brunch

Surprise someone you love with a very private May Day breakfast in bed, or deliver colorful spring flowers to the doorsteps of friends early May Day morning with an invitation to brunch in your backyard or on the patio. This menu is specifically designed for an at-home picnic with access to normal cooking facilities. If outdoor electrical outlets are available, enjoy the fresh morning air on the patio where guests can watch the cook at work.

To simplify cooking procedures in the morning, almost everything in this menu can be partially or completely prepared the night before. Even the crêpes can be cooked, stacked and refrigerated prior to reheating in a warm oven just before filling and serving. Besides last-minute mixing of the Champagne Daisies, only the Beef and Egg Rolls and biscuits require on-the-spot preparation.

CHAMPAGNE DAISIES

2 cups fresh orange juice   orange slices
1 quart club soda   fresh mint sprigs
1 bottle champagne or
     sparkling white wine

1. Combine orange juice, club soda and champagne in a large pitcher just before serving.

2. Pour over cracked ice in wine glasses and garnish with an orange slice and a sprig of mint.

Yield: about 10 cups

SPARKLING ORANGE JUICE

1   quart fresh orange juice   orange slices
1½ quarts sparkling water   fresh mint sprigs

1. Combine orange juice and sparkling water in a large pitcher just before serving.

2. Pour over cracked ice in wine glasses and garnish each serving with an orange slice and a sprig of mint.

Yield: 10 cups

GINGERED VEGETABLE MEDLEY

A tangy cold vegetable salad!

one 10-ounce package
     frozen baby carrots
one 10-ounce package
     frozen tiny peas
one 8-ounce can water
     chestnuts, drained
¾ cup orange juice
¼ cup sherry (substitute
     additional ¼ cup
     orange juice if desired)

1 teaspoon grated fresh
     ginger, or
   ½ teaspoon ground
     ginger
salt and pepper to taste
½ cup slivered almonds

1. Combine all ingredients except the almonds in a heavy skillet. Carefully break apart carrots and peas if necessary.

2. Cover and bring to a boil. Simmer 3 to 5 minutes, until the carrots are barely tender.

3. Transfer vegetables and cooking liquid to a salad bowl. Cover and chill.

4. To serve, lift vegetables from the liquid and arrange in a serving bowl. Sprinkle with slivered almonds.

Serves 6

COTTAGE CHEESE CONFETTI

2 cups small curd cottage
     cheese
¼ cup finely diced
     cucumber
¼ cup finely diced celery
¼ cup thinly sliced radishes
2 scallions, finely sliced
     (including part of the
     green tops)

2 tablespoons finely
     snipped fresh parsley
salt and pepper to taste
1 teaspoon Worcestershire
     sauce
dash of cayenne pepper
Tomato Shells (page 92)

1. Combine cottage cheese with remaining ingredients except Tomato Shells, and mix well.

2. Serve in Tomato Shells.

Yield: 3 cups or enough to fill 6 medium-size tomato shells

Variation: Serve in lettuce cups or green pepper cases.

BEEF AND EGG ROLLS

4 tablespoons butter or margarine
1 small onion, finely chopped
6 to 8 fresh mushrooms, finely chopped
6 eggs, beaten
salt and pepper to taste

12 thin slices cold rare roast beef, each about 4 × 8 inches
6 slices Muenster cheese, cut into thin strips
2 to 4 tablespoons butter or margarine

1. Melt 4 tablespoons butter in a large heavy skillet. Add onion and mushrooms and sauté quickly. Add more butter if necessary.

2. Add beaten eggs and salt and pepper to taste. Mix well and cook until eggs are set, stirring continually. Remove from heat.

3. For each roll, overlap the long edges of two pieces of roast beef to form an approximate square. Spoon scrambled egg mixture into the center of each square, then add cheese strips. Fold the edges of meat over the eggs and roll up securely.

4. Melt 2 to 4 tablespoons butter in a heavy skillet and place beef rolls in the butter, seam side down. Brown on all sides. Lift from pan and drain.

5. Serve warm or chilled with Dipping Sauce (page 48), or tuck into hot dog rolls and garnish with ketchup, mustard and relish.

Serves 6

FRESH PEACH CREPES

1 recipe Almond Crêpes (page 57)
¾ cup ricotta cheese
¾ cup sugar
¼ teaspoon vanilla
2 teaspoons Amaretto liqueur or
   ¾ teaspoon almond extract

½ cup heavy cream, whipped
2 fresh peaches, peeled, pitted and sliced
chopped slivered almonds
shavings of semisweet chocolate

1. Prepare crêpes following the directions given below. Stack cooked crêpes and place them in a warm oven, or make them ahead of time, stack, refrigerate and reheat in a warm oven when ready to serve.

2. Combine ricotta, sugar, vanilla and Amaretto or almond extract, and beat until smooth. Fold in whipped cream. Cover and refrigerate.

3. When ready to serve, spoon cheese mixture into the center of each crêpe, add peach slices, reserving a few for garnish, then bring edges of the crepe to the center to overlap filling. Place two filled crêpes on each plate and spoon additional cheese mixture over the top. Garnish with reserved peach slices, chopped almonds and chocolate shavings.

Serves 6 to 8

Variations: Substitute any fresh or well-drained canned fruit for the peaches.

PICNIC NOTE: This is a very special dessert meant for special, at-home picnics. Do not assemble crêpes ahead of time as the fruit juices will run, causing soggy crêpes. The ingredients for these could conceivably be carried to a picnic and assembled, but the cheese mixture must be kept thoroughly chilled until you're ready to use it. Prepare and cook the crêpes just before leaving home and stack them between layers of waxed paper. Then wrap them in aluminum foil to keep them warm, or serve them cold.

ALMOND CREPES

1 cup all-purpose flour	¼ teaspoon almond extract
1 tablespoon sugar	2 eggs
½ cup milk	2 egg yolks
½ cup water	1 tablespoon butter, melted
4 tablespoons ground toasted, slivered almonds	vegetable oil

1. Sift flour into a mixing bowl and add sugar, milk, water, ground almonds and almond extract. Stir until smooth.

2. Beat eggs and egg yolks together and add to the flour mixture. Add melted butter and beat mixture until smooth. Cover and refrigerate 1 hour.

3. To cook crêpes, wipe a 6-inch crêpe pan with oil and heat the pan until it is hot. Pour 2 tablespoons of batter into the hot pan, then quickly tilt the pan so that the batter covers the bottom of the pan. Cook over high heat.

4. When crêpe forms slight bubbles, loosen the edges and, when crêpe is lightly browned, carefully turn with a spatula to cook the other side. As each crêpe is completed, stack it on a plate.

5. To serve, fill the center of each crêpe with your favorite fruit filling or ice cream, then fold edges to overlap in the center and top with a sauce or syrup.

Yield: 12 to 18 crêpes

Moving Day Picnic

For many people, one of the most difficult tasks associated with moving is making new friends. New neighbors would love to be welcomed to their home with a picnic lunch planned in their honor. So the next time the moving van pulls up in your neighborhood, greet the new arrivals with this hearty picnic lunch. (Special neighbors who are moving away would also welcome it as a parting gift!)

Everything in the menu can be prepared ahead of time and the stew can be kept warm in an attractive wide-mouthed thermal container or newspaper-wrapped casserole dish so your new neighbors won't have to worry about trying to get the stove hooked up in order to enjoy their first warm meal in new surroundings. And their warm smiles of thanks are bound to be the beginning of new friendships and neighborly picnic outings in the future. Since it's often difficult to locate the exact box (or boxes) containing the dinnerware, be sure to include throwaway paper plates and cups. Tuck in bright paper napkins and a matching paper tablecloth to drape over a moving carton for a makeshift table on which to spread the lunch.

HEARTY BEEF AND BEER STEW

2 pounds lean beef	1 tablespoon dried basil
¼ cup peanut oil	½ teaspoon dried thyme
½ cup all-purpose flour	1 tablespoon salt
1 medium-size onion, sliced ¼ inch thick	one 10½-ounce can beef consommé
3 cloves garlic, minced	1 cup beer
2 tablespoons brown sugar	1 tablespoon red wine vinegar
¼ cup chopped fresh parsley	
1 bay leaf	

1. Preheat oven to 325°F.

2. Trim any fat from beef. Cut beef into 2-inch cubes.

3. Heat peanut oil in a large skillet.

4. Dredge the meat in the flour and brown in the heated oil, doing only a few pieces at a time. Place browned beef in a casserole and add onion.

5. Brown garlic in the oil remaining in the skillet. Add brown sugar, parsley, bay leaf, basil, thyme, salt, consommé and beer.

6. Pour mixture over the meat and onions in the casserole, cover and bake for 2½ hours.

7. Uncover, add red wine vinegar and return to oven until bubbly on top.

Serves 4 to 6

PICNIC NOTE: Transport in a wide-mouthed thermal container or wrap the casserole dish in newspaper and a towel; be sure to pack a serving scoop.

ZUCCHINI SALAD

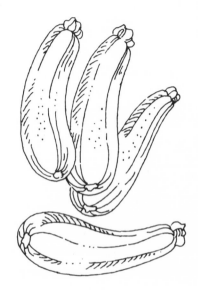

4	small zucchini, thinly sliced	3	tablespoons red wine vinegar
½	cup finely sliced scallions (including part of the green tops)	1	tablespoon Dijon-style mustard
½	cup thinly sliced celery	1	clove garlic, finely minced
¾	cup thinly sliced radishes	1	teaspoon salt
1	green pepper, seeded and thinly sliced	½	teaspoon pepper
		1	teaspoon sugar
⅓	cup olive oil	½	teaspoon dried oregano
			lettuce leaves

1. Place vegetables in a large bowl.

2. Place remaining ingredients in a shaker jar and shake vigorously to mix well.

3. Pour over vegetables and allow to marinate at room temperature for at least 1 hour.

4. Serve over lettuce leaves.

Serves 6

FRESH FRUIT WITH HONEY YOGURT

I can make a whole meal of this delicious salad. Change the fresh fruit ingredients as new ones come into season throughout the spring and summer.

2	cups plain yogurt	sliced peaches
¼	cup honey	fresh blueberries
2	teaspoons grated lemon rind	sliced apples (with skin)
		chunks of cantaloupe
2	tablespoons lemon juice	raisins (optional)
½	teaspoon vanilla	coarsely chopped walnuts (optional)
	sliced strawberries	
	sliced bananas	shredded coconut (optional)

1. In a small bowl combine the yogurt with honey, lemon rind and juice, and vanilla. Cover and chill.

2. To serve, fill bowls with mixed fresh fruit and cover with Honey Yogurt. Sprinkle with raisins, walnuts and coconut, if desired.

Yield: dressing for 6 servings of mixed fruit

PICNIC NOTE: Mix the yogurt dressing, chill and pack in a small thermal container. Prepare the fruit, mix it together, and carry it to the picnic in an airtight plastic container.

CHEESE BISCUITS

2¼ cups sifted all-purpose flour	½ cup margarine
4 teaspoons baking powder	½ cup grated sharp Cheddar cheese
1 teaspoon salt	1 cup milk

1. Preheat oven to 450°F.

2. Blend flour, baking powder and salt together in a medium-size bowl.

3. Cut in margarine with pastry blender or fork. Mixture should be crumbly. Mix in cheese.

4. Stir in almost all the milk to make a pliable dough which will be easy to roll out. Add more milk if necessary. Dough should not be sticky.

5. Turn dough out onto a lightly floured surface and knead gently, about 30 seconds.

6. Roll the dough out to ½-inch thickness and cut with floured biscuit cutter.

7. Bake on an ungreased baking sheet for 12 to 15 minutes or until light golden brown.

Yield: about thirty 1½-inch biscuits

CHOCOLATE MARBLED BUTTERSCOTCH BROWNIES

Brownie Mixture

1	cup butter or margarine	4	eggs
2	cups light brown sugar, firmly packed	1½	cups all-purpose flour
		1	teaspoon baking powder
one	6-ounce package butterscotch chips, melted and cooled 5 minutes	2	teaspoons vanilla
		1	cup chopped pecans

Marble Filling

two	3-ounce packages cream cheese	2	eggs
one	1-ounce square unsweetened chocolate, melted and cooled 5 minutes	⅓	cup dark brown sugar, firmly packed
		2	tablespoons cocoa
		2	tablespoons flour
¼	cup butter or margarine	1	tablespoon vanilla

1. To make brownie mixture, cream butter until fluffy, then beat in sugar. Add melted butterscotch chips and beat until well blended.

2. Add eggs, one at a time, and beat 1 minute after each addition.

3. Stir in flour, baking powder, vanilla and pecans, and mix well. Divide half of the mixture between two greased 8 × 8-inch baking pans. Set aside the remaining brownie mixture.

4. Preheat oven to 350°F.

5. To make marble filling, place cream cheese, melted chocolate and butter in a medium-size bowl and cream until mixture is light and fluffy.

6. Beat in eggs, then add remaining ingredients and mix well. Divide mixture between the two pans of brownie mixture and spread over the top carefully.

7. Divide reserved brownie mixture between the two pans and spread over the chocolate layer. Pull a knife through the layered mixtures in deep, wide curves to create a marbled appearance. Bake for 45 to 50 minutes or until toothpick inserted in the center comes out clean.

8. Cool and frost, if desired, with Maple Cream or Chocolate Cream Frosting (page 193).

9. Cut into squares.

Yield: 12 to 18 brownies

Bridal Shower Picnic Buffet

Besides the flowers, spring brings lots of parties for June brides. Take advantage of the warming trend to plan a backyard bridal shower for a special friend. The menu here revolves around a large colorful fruit salad which can almost be a meal in itself. Stuffed Lobster Tails make a special entrée for such an occasion to be followed by a sweet confection for dessert with almond-flavored iced coffee. Of course, the gift should be a picnic basket! Ask guests to bring a gift suitable for outfitting a pretty wicker picnic basket which you provide.

CURRIED VEGETABLE PATE

3 tablespoons butter
½ cup finely chopped onion
⅓ pound fresh mushrooms, chopped
1 teaspoon dried basil
½ teaspoon capers
1½ teaspoons lemon juice
⅛ teaspoon garlic powder
½ teaspoon salt
dash of pepper
½ teaspoon mild curry powder (or hot curry, if you prefer)
½ cup snipped fresh parsley
one 9-ounce package frozen French-style green beans, cooked and cooled
2 hard-cooked eggs, cooled, peeled and chopped
2 tablespoons Mayonnaise (page 190)
cherry tomatoes
snipped fresh parsley

1. Melt butter in a heavy skillet. Add onion, mushrooms and basil, and sauté.

2. Add capers, lemon juice, garlic powder, salt, pepper, curry powder and parsley, and mix well. Remove from heat. Cool.

3. Chop cooked and cooled green beans. Then add beans and eggs to the onion-mushroom mixture. Fold in Mayonnaise.

4. Put pâté mixture through food grinder with fine blade, or process in blender. Add up to 2 tablespoons sherry or water if extra moisture is needed in blender jar.

5. Line a 2-cup mold or bowl with transparent wrap and spoon pâté into lined mold. Cover and chill to mellow for at least a day.

6. To serve, unmold onto serving dish and garnish with halved cherry tomatoes and snipped parsley. Spread on crackers or rounds of bread.

Yield: 2 cups

DEEP FRIED CHEESE BALLS

1½ cups grated American or Cheddar cheese	1 tablespoon all-purpose flour
¼ teaspoon salt	3 egg whites, stiffly beaten
dash of Tabasco sauce (or more to your liking)	½ cup fine bread or cracker crumbs
½ teaspoon dry mustard	vegetable oil
	Mustard Sauce (page 111)

1. Combine cheese with salt, Tabasco, mustard and flour.

2. Fold in beaten egg whites. Shape mixture into walnut-size balls. Roll in crumbs. Allow to sit 5 minutes.

3. Heat oil to 350°F in deep saucepan. Fry cheese balls a few at a time until golden brown. Drain on absorbent paper.

4. Serve hot or cold with Mustard Sauce.

Yield: 24 to 30 appetizers

FRUIT SALAD TOSS-UP

This salad is a new twist on the traditional Chef Salad and is particularly appropriate for a spring or summer backyard picnic/ bridal shower.

4 cups mixed salad greens (try iceberg or Boston lettuce and watercress, or any other favorite combination)	1 cup blueberries, raspberries or strawberries
4 medium-size oranges	1 pound sliced Swiss or Jarlsberg cheese, cut into match-thin strips
1 medium-size cantaloupe	1 pound sliced boiled ham, cut into match-thin strips
1 pound seedless green grapes	1 whole chicken breast, cooked and shredded
2 small to medium-size crisp red apples	Orange and Onion Dressing (page 64)
lemon juice	
1 large avocado, peeled, pitted and sliced	

1. Wash greens well and tear into bite-size pieces. Line a large bowl with the prepared greens. Refrigerate.

2. Remove peel and outer membrane from oranges. Break oranges into sections.

3. Cut cantaloupe in half, remove seeds, and prepare melon balls using a melon baller, or cut the fruit into bite-size chunks.

4. Cut each grape in half lengthwise.

5. Wash apples and chop. Do not remove skin. Sprinkle with lemon juice. Sprinkle avocado slices with lemon juice. Wash berries and allow to drain. (Cut strawberries in half lengthwise.)

6. Arrange fruit, cheese, ham and chicken in the greens-lined salad bowl and toss with Orange and Onion Dressing.

Serves 6

PICNIC NOTE: Most of the ingredients for this salad can be prepared ahead of time and stored in individual airtight containers if the picnic is to be carried. Prepare apple and avocado at picnic to avoid extensive discoloration prior to serving.

ORANGE AND ONION DRESSING

1 teaspoon onion juice
2 teaspoons grated orange rind
¼ cup red wine vinegar
½ teaspoon salt
½ teaspoon dry mustard
2 tablespoons brown sugar
¼ cup olive or corn oil
¼ cup dairy sour cream

1. Prepare onion juice by squeezing small pieces of raw onion in a garlic press held over a small bowl.

2. Measure all ingredients except sour cream into a small bowl and beat together with a rotary beater until creamy.

3. Add sour cream and beat until smooth. Cover and refrigerate until serving time.

Yield: ¾ cup

PICNIC NOTE: This dressing is especially good over a mixed fruit salad. Don't toss with salad fixings until just before serving time, or allow each picnicker to serve and toss her or his own.

STUFFED LOBSTER TAILS

6   lobster tails
1   cup fresh crabmeat
6   large fresh mushrooms,
      finely chopped
one   8-ounce can water
      chestnuts, finely minced
½-inch   piece fresh ginger,
      peeled and finely
      chopped

2   tablespoons fine dry
      bread crumbs
½   teaspoon salt
½   teaspoon sugar
2   tablespoons chicken bouillon
dash of white pepper
1   tablespoon peanut or
      sesame oil

1. Split lobster tails lengthwise and put in cold water for 5 minutes. Drain. Slip meat out of shells and chop meat finely. Set empty shells aside.

2. Mix chopped lobster with remaining ingredients and stuff mixture back into the lobster shells with a wet spoon.

3. Place stuffed shells on a rack in a pan of boiling water, cover and steam for 10 to 15 minutes, until stuffing is heated through. Remove and serve immediately or chill and serve cold with Dipping Sauce (page 48).

Serves 6

COLD CAULIFLOWER NIVERNAIS

2   small- to medium-size
      heads cauliflower
1¼   cups Mayonnaise
      (page 190)
¼   cup plus 2 tablespoons
      dairy sour cream

¼   cup Dijon-style mustard
salt and freshly ground
      pepper to taste
fresh parsley sprigs

1. Break cauliflower into flowerets and cook, covered, in boiling salted water for 7 minutes. Drain, then plunge into ice water to stop cooking action. Drain.

2. Combine remaining ingredients except parsley and beat with a wire whisk or rotary beater until light and creamy.

3. Pour sauce over the cauliflower, garnish with the parsley and chill thoroughly.

Serves 6

NUT-FILLED BUTTERHORNS

Butterhorns

4 cups sifted all-purpose flour	¼ cup warm water (110° to 115°F)
1 tablespoon sugar	
1 teaspoon salt	4 egg yolks at room temperature
1 cup butter or margarine, softened	½ cup cultured sour cream, scalded and cooled to lukewarm
2 packages active dry yeast	

Filling

4 egg whites	1 cup finely chopped walnuts
1 cup granulated sugar	confectioners' sugar
1 teaspoon vanilla	

1. To make butterhorns, mix flour, sugar and salt together in a large mixing bowl. Cut butter into the flour mixture with a pastry blender or fork. Mixture should resemble coarse meal.

2. Dissolve yeast in warm water. Add yeast to flour mixture and blend well.

3. Stir egg yolks into lukewarm sour cream, then fold into flour and yeast mixture. Mix well.

4. Place waxed paper over the dough, then wrap in a cloth or aluminum foil and chill for 3 to 24 hours. This is a rich dough which will not rise very much.

5. To make filling (just before removing dough from the refrigerator), beat egg whites to the soft peak stage, then gradually beat in the granulated sugar and vanilla. Beat again until stiff. Gently fold in the walnuts.

6. Preheat oven to 375°F.

7. Remove dough from refrigerator and divide into eight parts. Roll out one at a time into 8-inch circles on a board or paper sprinkled with confectioners' sugar. (Refrigerate the sections not being used.)

8. Cover circle of dough with a thin layer of filling, then cut into eight wedges. Roll up, beginning at the wide edge, and place on an ungreased baking sheet. Bake until golden brown, 15 to 20 minutes. Remove from pan and cool on rack.

9. Roll in confectioners' sugar before serving if desired.

Yield: 64 butterhorns

ICED CAFETA

Amaretto liqueur and cream make this an exceptional iced coffee drink. See the variation for a nonalcoholic version.

1 quart strong hot coffee	3 to 4 tablespoons
1 cup sugar	Amaretto liqueur (or
⅛ teaspoon ground mace	more, to your liking)
⅛ teaspoon ground allspice	whipped cream (optional)
¼ cup cream or condensed milk	

1. Combine coffee with sugar, mace and allspice. Let mixture stand until cool.

2. Stir in the cream and Amaretto. Refrigerate.

3. Serve over cracked ice with a dollop of whipped cream if desired.

Yield: 4½ cups

Variation: If you prefer a nonalcoholic version of this iced drink, substitute ¼ teaspoon almond extract for the Amaretto and stir in ¼ cup ground almonds. Strain through cheesecloth; refrigerate.

Summer Spreads

For Mountains, Seashore and Backyard

Summer Supper Chic

This elegant picnic is perfect for lovers on a private celebration. A bottle of iced champagne or sparkling wine (don't forget the corkscrew) complements the tasty cold Herbed Cornish Game Hens and Artichoke Quiche.

The recipes included in this picnic are scaled to serve four to six. If this menu is used for two, the dishes can be divided into individual portions, and the extras stored away for later enjoyment. The quiche and the pie would be particularly attractive made in individual tart pans. Use small thermal containers to hold servings of soup and coffee.

PEACHY CANTALOUPE SOUP

1	medium-size ripe cantaloupe, peeled, cubed and chilled	¼	cup orange juice
		½	cup dry sherry (or substitute additional ½ cup orange juice)
2	ripe peaches, peeled, pitted and diced, or 4 canned peach halves	3	tablespoons orange rind
		3	tablespoons honey

1. Purée the ingredients together in batches in a blender jar.

2. Mix batches together in a large bowl, cover with transparent wrap and chill.

Yield: 5 to 6 cups

COLD HERBED CORNISH GAME HENS

four	1- to 1½-pound Cornish game hens	½	teaspoon dried thyme leaves
4	cloves garlic	½	teaspoon rubbed sage
4	bay leaves	¼	teaspoon powdered oregano
6	tablespoons butter or margarine	¼	teaspoon powdered marjoram
1½	teaspoons salt	½	teaspoon dried basil
1	teaspoon white pepper		fresh parsley sprigs
			lime slices

1. Rinse game hens and pat dry with paper towels. Rub skin of each hen with a cut clove of garlic, then place garlic clove and one bay leaf in cavity of each hen.

2. Melt butter in small saucepan and add remaining ingredients.

3. Place 1 tablespoon of the herb butter in each hen, then tie legs together.

4. Brush hens generously with herb butter and place, breast down, on a wire rack in a shallow baking pan. Place in a cold oven on the top shelf and then set the oven at 400°F. Bake 30 minutes, then turn hens, baste with additional herb butter and bake an additional 30 to 45 minutes, until the skin is golden brown, juices run clear and the meat is no longer pink when slashed near the bone. Cover and chill. Garnish with sprigs of fresh parsley and slices of lime if desired.

Serves 4 to 6

ARTICHOKE QUICHE

1 recipe Single Crust Pastry (page 188)	4 eggs
two 6-ounce jars marinated artichoke hearts	¼ cup half and half, milk or cream
3 scallions, chopped (including part of the green tops)	¼ pound Swiss cheese, grated
	1 to 2 tablespoons chopped fresh parsley
1 clove garlic, minced	dash of Tabasco sauce

1. Preheat oven to 425°F.

2. Prepare pastry according to directions on page 188. Roll out to a 12-inch circle on a lightly floured surface. Fit into a 9-inch pie plate. Trim overhang, turn under and flute edges and prick shell all over with fork. Bake for 8 minutes. Remove and cool slightly.

3. Decrease oven temperature to 375°F.

4. Drain the oil from the artichoke hearts into a heavy skillet. Heat the oil and sauté the scallions and garlic.

5. Beat eggs with half and half, then stir in the remaining ingredients.

6. Pour mixture into prepared pastry shell. Bake for 30 to 40 minutes or until set but still soft. Remove from oven and allow to set at least 15 minutes before slicing and serving.

Serves 6

AVOCADO AND GRAPEFRUIT SALAD

1	large head leaf lettuce	3	tablespoons lime juice
1	large head leaf lettuce	¾	teaspoon salt
1	large stalk celery, thinly sliced		dash of pepper
4	scallions, thinly sliced (including part of the green tops)	1	large ripe avocado, peeled, halved, pitted and sliced
1	small green pepper, seeded and finely chopped		lime juice
½	pound crabmeat (optional)	1	large pink grapefruit, peeled and sectioned
		4 to 6	tablespoons butter

1. Wash lettuce leaves and pat dry with paper towels. Use leaves to line a large salad bowl, then fill with the remaining leaves broken into bite-size pieces.

2. Mix celery, scallions and green pepper with crabmeat (if desired), 3 tablespoons lime juice, the salt and pepper. Add to lettuce and toss lightly.

3. Just before serving, prepare avocado and sprinkle with a little additional lime juice, then arrange with grapefruit sections on top of the salad.

4. Melt butter in a small heavy saucepan, *shaking the pan continually,* for 2 or 3 minutes, until butter foams and turns golden brown.

5. Pour butter over salad, toss lightly and serve immediately.

Serves 6

Variation: Substitute Vinaigrette Dressing (page 190) for browned butter.

PICNIC NOTE: Prepare salad through Step 2, then place on ice (see page 13). Pack butter in a small butter melter. Complete salad preparation at picnic just before serving.

BUTTERHORNS

½	cup butter or margarine	3	eggs, beaten
1	cup milk	4 to 4½	cups sifted all-purpose flour
½	cup sugar		melted butter
1	teaspoon salt		
1	package active dry yeast		

1. Melt ½ cup butter in a saucepan. Add milk and heat mixture to between 110° and 115°F.

2. Pour warm milk mixture over sugar and salt in a large mixing bowl. Add yeast and mix well.

3. Stir in beaten eggs. Add flour gradually and mix to a smooth, soft dough.

4. Knead dough lightly on a lightly floured surface. Place dough in a clean, lightly greased bowl and cover with a slightly damp tea towel. Set to rise in a warm place* until doubled, about 1 hour.

5. Divide dough into thirds. Roll each section into a 9-inch circle on a floured surface. Lightly brush circle with melted butter. Cut into wedges and roll into crescents starting at the wide end.

6. Place crescents on greased baking sheets and curve ends in. Lightly brush with melted butter, cover with a clean towel and set to rise in a warm place until almost doubled, about 30 minutes.

7. Preheat oven to 400°F.

8. Bake for 12 to 15 minutes or until golden brown.

9. Serve warm or cooled with butter and/or preserves.

Yield: 24 to 30 butterhorns

CHOCOLATE PECAN PIE

1 recipe Single Crust Pastry (page 188)	½ teaspoon vanilla
½ cup evaporated milk	1 tablespoon brandy (optional)
one 6-ounce package semi-sweet chocolate pieces	½ cup light brown sugar, packed
3 eggs	1 cup coarsely chopped pecans

1. Prepare pastry according to directions on page 188. Roll out to a 12-inch circle on a lightly floured surface. Fit into a 9-inch pie plate. Trim overhang and turn under and flute edges. Set aside.

2. Preheat oven to 350°F.

3. In the top of a double boiler, combine milk and chocolate. Heat over medium heat until chocolate has melted and the sauce is smooth. Cool.

4. Beat eggs slightly. Add cooled chocolate sauce, vanilla and brandy (if desired). Blend in brown sugar, then add pecans and pour into the prepared pastry. Bake for 40 minutes. Chill.

Serves 6 to 8

*If you cannot find a draft-free warm spot in your kitchen, heat your oven to 400°F for 2 minutes, then turn it off and wrap the bowl containing the dough in a clean towel and place it in the oven to rise.

Lawn Concert Supper

A lawn concert is one of the most pleasant evening outings, with the warm night air erasing all thoughts of chilly winter winds. The menu for this summer picnic supper features quiche-like Pear and Potato Pie flecked with prosciutto, a perfect complement for cold Steak au Poivre and Armenian Country Salad. Start the meal with icy sherry spritzers or a unique basil drink and creamy Avocado Nut Butter followed by a cold soup. The grand finale is the very best pound cake I've ever tasted. It's the author's choice for the *best* recipe in this book. Just read the ingredients—you'll love it before you taste it!

SHERRY-CIDER SPRITZERS

For each serving:

2 ounces dry cocktail sherry
3 ounces apple cider or juice

crushed ice
club soda

1. Pour sherry and cider over crushed ice.
2. Fill glass with club soda.

SWEET BASIL JULEP

A nonalcoholic "julep" for hot summer thirsts.

2 tablespoons finely minced
   fresh basil leaves
¾ cup sugar
juice of 2 lemons
juice of 1 large orange

1 cup cold water
one 32-ounce bottle ginger
   ale or lemon-lime soda,
   thoroughly chilled
fresh basil sprigs

1. Mix minced basil with sugar and fruit juices. Allow mixture to stand 2 hours.
2. Add water and chilled ginger ale and mix well.
3. Serve over cracked ice. Garnish with sprigs of fresh basil.

Yield: 6 servings

Variations: Substitute mint leaves for the basil for a true julep taste. For an alcoholic version, substitute bourbon for the soda.

PICNIC NOTE: Prepare the basil "syrup" prior to the picnic and carry in a 2-quart thermal container with the water. Add ginger ale just before serving at the picnic.

AVOCADO NUT BUTTER

1 large ripe avocado, peeled, halved and pitted	4 ounces cream cheese
juice of 1 lime	1 teaspoon ground ginger
1 cup butter	1 cup dry-roasted sunflower nuts

1. Cut avocado into small chunks, place in medium-size mixing bowl and beat to purée, or process in blender.

2. Add lime juice. Beat in butter, cream cheese and ginger. Chill until firm.

3. Roll butter into ball on waxed paper, then roll in sunflower nuts to coat. Chill.

4. Serve as a cocktail ball with crackers.

Yield: ¾ pound

PICNIC NOTE: Try this delicately flavored butter as a sandwich spread with ham or turkey on rye or pumpernickel. Or make a batch with sunflower seeds mixed in and freeze it in small tubs or crocks to use as a butter for baked potatoes.

COLD CARROT AND APPLE SOUP

1 pound carrots, peeled and cut into 2-inch lengths	2 tablespoons brandy (optional)
1 quart apple juice or apple cider	¼ cup brown sugar, packed
3 tablespoons butter	½ teaspoon nutmeg
3 large tart apples, peeled, cored and chopped	½ teaspoon cinnamon
1 small red onion, finely chopped	¼ teaspoon ground cloves
	yogurt
	raisins

1. Combine carrots with apple juice in a medium-size saucepan. Bring to a boil, then simmer until carrots are tender, adding water or more apple juice as necessary to cover.

2. Melt butter in a large heavy skillet. Sauté apples and onion until soft and caramely. Stir in brandy (if desired), sugar, nutmeg, cinnamon and cloves.

3. Purée carrots and apple juice with sautéed apple mixture in a blender. Cover and chill.

4. Serve with a dollop of yogurt and a few raisins sprinkled on top.

Yield: 5 to 6 cups

STEAK AU POIVRE

Prepare this well ahead of time so it has time to chill, or enjoy it hot from the picnic grill. Just choose the appropriate cooking method listed below.

6 club steaks, or one 4-pound sirloin steak, 2 inches thick Dijon-style mustard	6 to 8 tablespoons peppercorns, coarsely ground (use the blender or coffee grinder)

Preparation

1. Wipe steak with damp paper towels. Coat one side of each steak with mustard, then press pepper into steak so that it is well coated to hold the juices in while cooking. Repeat on other side.

2. Let stand at least 1 hour at room temperature but no longer than 2 hours.

Cooking Method 1

1. Melt 6 tablespoons butter in a heavy skillet. Sear steak for about 6 minutes on each side to form a crust which seals in the spice. The inside should be rare. Cool, then refrigerate.

2. Slice thickly to serve alone or with Cumberland Sauce (below).

Cooking Method 2

1. Grill steaks about 5 inches from hot coals for 5 to 6 minutes on each side. Test for doneness.

2. Remove to serving platter or individual plates.

3. To serve, sprinkle each steak with salt and a little lemon juice and dot with butter. Garnish with fresh parsley.

Serves 6

PICNIC NOTE: If you choose Cooking Method 2, coat steaks with mustard and pepper prior to picnic packing and place on a large platter. Wrap in foil and place in cooler for at least 1 hour before grilling.

CUMBERLAND SAUCE

1½ cups red currant jelly	⅓ cup orange juice
1 teaspoon finely chopped shallot	¼ cup lemon juice
peel from ½ orange and ½ lemon	1 cup Port wine
	1 teaspoon Dijon-style mustard

1. Combine jelly and shallot in a small saucepan and cook over low heat until jelly is melted.

2. Cut the orange and lemon peels into long, thin strips and blanch in boiling water for 2 or 3 minutes. Drain and add to liquefied jelly.

3. Combine remaining ingredients and add to jelly mixture. Mix well and cool.

Yield: about 3 cups

PEAR AND POTATO PIE

2 medium-size potatoes, peeled and thinly sliced	½ teaspoon salt
1 recipe Double Crust Pastry (page 188)	1½ teaspoons dried basil
	2 tablespoons finely chopped onion
2 ripe but firm medium-size pears, peeled and thinly sliced	2 eggs, lightly beaten
	½ cup milk
8 to 10 paper-thin slices prosciutto	2 tablespoons flour
	sour cream (optional)

1. Place sliced potatoes in salted water to cover. Let stand at room temperature while you prepare remaining ingredients.

2. Preheat oven to 375°F.

3. Prepare pastry according to directions on page 188. Divide dough into two approximately equal portions, then roll the larger portion out to a 12-inch circle on a lightly floured surface. Fit into a 9-inch pie plate. Trim overhang. Set aside.

4. Drain and rinse potatoes and pat dry with paper towels. Place in medium-size mixing bowl with sliced pears.

5. Cut prosciutto into thin strips and add to potatoes and pears along with salt, basil and onion. Mix well. Transfer mixture to pastry-lined pie plate.

6. In a small bowl, mix beaten eggs, milk, and flour together and pour over potato mixture.

7. Prepare top crust by rolling out remaining dough to a 10-inch circle. Make several slits in the crust to allow steam to escape during baking. Cover potato mixture, trim overhang, turn under and flute edges of pastry. Bake for about 55 minutes or until lightly browned.

8. Serve at room temperature or cold with sour cream if desired.

Serves 6

ARMENIAN COUNTRY SALAD

one 15-ounce can red kidney beans, drained	½ to ¾ cup finely chopped fresh parsley
one 15-ounce can chick peas, drained	16 cherry tomatoes, halved
1 small onion, finely chopped	1 recipe Vinaigrette Dressing (page 190)
1 small green pepper, seeded and chopped	¼ to ½ pound Feta cheese, crumbled

1. Combine kidney beans, chick peas, onion, green pepper, parsley, tomatoes and Vinaigrette Dressing in large bowl and mix well. Refrigerate.

2. Bring salad to room temperature to serve. Sprinkle with crumbled cheese.

Serves 6

CREAM CHEESE POUND CAKE

1 cup margarine	3 cups sugar
½ cup butter	6 eggs
one 8-ounce package cream cheese	3 cups sifted all-purpose flour
	1 tablespoon vanilla

1. Preheat oven to 325°F.

2. In a very large mixing bowl, cream margarine, butter and cream cheese together until light and fluffy. (Place mixing bowl in sink during entire mixing process to avoid spattering the mixture all over the kitchen.)

3. Add sugar to mixture and blend well.

4. Add 2 of the eggs, beat well, then add 1 cup of the flour and beat well. Repeat with remaining eggs and flour, beating well after each addition.

5. Add vanilla and mix well.

6. Spoon cake batter into well-greased and floured 10-inch tube pan. Bake for 1 hour and 25 minutes, until golden brown and toothpick inserted in center comes out clean. ABSOLUTELY NO PEEKING during baking period. Allow cake to cool in pan for 10 minutes, then invert pan and remove cake to wire rack to cool.

7. Serve plain or with Rhubarb Sauce (page 193).

Serves 10 to 20

Fourth of July Family Barbecue

Celebrate the Fourth with a family-style evening barbecue in the backyard or a nearby park with an ideal vantage point for watching fireworks displays when the sun sets. Who can resist the tempting aromas of traditional favorites, chicken and ribs cooked over coals, accompanied by potato salad, coleslaw and corn on the cob? And what could be a more patriotic way to end the meal than to indulge in ice cream handcranked on the spot with each picnicker doing his or her share to produce the all-time favorite American dessert?

CHERRY TOMATO DIPPERS

Cherry tomatoes add color (and vitamins) to almost any picnic meal. Packed in a loaf of dark pumpernickel bread, they make a colorful centerpiece.

one 1-pound round loaf dark pumpernickel bread	1 pint basket cherry tomatoes, stemmed Blue Cheese Dip (below)

1. Cut a healthy slice from the top of the loaf of pumpernickel and carefully remove the interior bread leaving the crust intact. Reserve removed bread for stuffing or other use.

2. Wash and dry cherry tomatoes and carefully pack them in the hollowed loaf. Replace top slice for lid.

3. Take along a tub of Blue Cheese Dip.

Serves 6

BLUE CHEESE DIP

1 cup plain yogurt	4 ounces blue cheese, crumbled
1 cup dairy sour cream	1 clove garlic, minced
2 tablespoons finely chopped scallions (including part of the green tops)	dash of pepper 1 tablespoon Worcestershire sauce

1. Combine all ingredients and mix well. Cover tightly; refrigerate.

2. Serve with cherry tomatoes and other raw vegetables.

Yield: 2 cups

STUFFED RAW MUSHROOMS

24 large fresh mushrooms
lemon juice
two 3-ounce packages
    cream cheese
¼ cup ricotta cheese
1 clove garlic, minced
2 beef bouillon cubes,
    powdered (whirl in
    blender)

2 teaspoons dried basil
1 teaspoon salt
pepper to taste
dash of Tabasco sauce
    (optional)
2 tablespoons finely
    chopped onion
finely snipped fresh parsley
    or chives

1. Clean mushrooms thoroughly and carefully remove the stems. Sprinkle inside of mushrooms with a little lemon juice.

2. Chop the mushroom stems finely, toss with a little lemon juice and set aside.

3. Soften cream cheese. Whip with ricotta, garlic, bouillon, basil, salt and pepper. Add a dash of Tabasco (if desired).

4. Fold in onion and chopped mushroom stems, and mix ingredients thoroughly.

5. Pack each mushroom cap with prepared filling, then invert onto snipped parsley or chives. Cover and refrigerate.

Yield: 24 appetizers

SALAMI-WRAPPED SCALLIONS

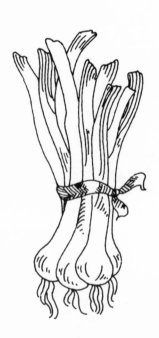

Traditional hors d'oeuvres make wonderful picnic finger food, easy to pack and easier to eat.

one 8-ounce package cream
    cheese
2 tablespoons chopped chives

24 paper-thin slices of
    salami, 3 inches in
    diameter
24 scallions

1. In a small bowl, whip cream cheese until light and fluffy. Add chives and mix well.

2. Spread a light layer of cream cheese mixture on each slice of salami.

3. Trim each scallion to about 5 inches in length. Place 1 scallion in the center of each salami slice and roll up. Secure with a toothpick. Cover and refrigerate until serving time.

Yield: 24 appetizers

Variations: Strips of dill pickle, canned asparagus tips or thin strips of zucchini can be substituted for the scallions.

FRUITED COLESLAW

1 large head cabbage	⅓ cup white wine vinegar
2 red Delicious apples	1½ teaspoons sugar
lemon juice	½ teaspoon salt
one 16-ounce can mandarin oranges	½ teaspoon celery seed
1 cup plain yogurt	freshly ground pepper to taste
1 cup dairy sour cream	

1. Finely shred enough of the cabbage to make 2 quarts.

2. Coarsely shred the unpeeled apples, sprinkle with lemon juice and toss with cabbage.

3. Drain and reserve the canning liquid from the mandarin oranges. Reserve 6 sections and chop the remaining oranges finely. Add to cabbage mixture.

4. Mix remaining ingredients together in small bowl, then pour over the cabbage mixture. If desired, moisten the slaw with a little of the reserved mandarin orange liquid. Garnish with reserved orange sections in a pinwheel design. Cover and chill.

Serves 10 to 12

PICNIC POTATO SALAD

No family picnic was ever complete without this tasty salad. The secret to really good potato salad is in the potato dicing. The finer the dice, the better the salad will be since the flavors will have a better chance to develop throughout the mixture.

6 medium-size red potatoes, boiled in their jackets and chilled	¾ cup sweet pickle relish
salt and pepper	1¼ cups Mayonnaise (page 190)
3 hard-cooked eggs, cooled, peeled and finely chopped	¼ cup ketchup
	3 tablespoons sugar
1 small- to medium-size onion, finely chopped	1¼ teaspoons salt
	¼ teaspoon pepper
3 large stalks celery, coarsely chopped	2 teaspoons prepared mustard

1. Remove jackets from potatoes. Dice potatoes finely and place in a large salad bowl. Lightly salt and pepper layers as each potato is diced and added to the bowl.

2. Add chopped eggs, onion, celery and pickle relish to potatoes and mix well. Cover tightly and refrigerate.

3. Combine remaining ingredients in a small bowl and mix well.

4. Fold dressing into potato mixture. Taste and adjust seasonings. Cover and chill for at least 1 hour before serving.

Serves 10 to 12

PICNIC NOTE: Due to the egg content, this salad must be chilled until serving time.

ROASTED CORN ON THE COB

Nothing says summer like fresh, charcoal-roasted corn on the cob. It's easy to prepare in one of the following ways.

Foil-Roasting

1. Remove corn husks and silk. For easy removal of the silk, rub the stripped ears with a dry terry cloth dishcloth or hand towel.

2. Cut sheets of heavy-duty aluminum foil large enough to accommodate each ear with plenty of foil for sealing the ear.

3. Mix softened butter (about ½ cup for every 6 ears) with salt and pepper to taste and a teaspoon or two of your favorite dried herb. Try rosemary, tarragon, basil, parsley or any combination.

4. Coat each ear of corn with the herb butter and wrap securely in the foil.

5. Place wrapped ears on the hot coals and cook for 15 minutes, turning often with tongs to avoid charring.

Husk-Roasting

1. Turn back husks on corn and carefully remove the silk. Return husks to original position.

2. Place corn on a grill over hot coals. Grill for about 20 minutes, turning often with tongs.

3. Serve with herb butter as described in Step 3, above.

BARBECUED CHICKEN

two	2½-pound frying chickens, cut up	1	recipe Chicken Barbecue Sauce (page 81)

1. Preheat oven to 350°F.

2. Wrap chicken pieces tightly in a large square of heavy-duty aluminum foil. Roast chicken in foil for 30 minutes.

3. Meanwhile, prepare Chicken Barbecue Sauce. Pour over partially cooked chicken. Cover, refrigerate and allow to marinate at least 4 hours.

4. Place chicken skin side up on the grill 4 to 6 inches from hot coals. Cook for about 20 minutes, turning and basting often with barbecue sauce.

Serves 6 to 8

CHICKEN BARBECUE SAUCE

one 10½-ounce can chicken broth	1 teaspoon brown sugar
	1 teaspoon salt
one 6-ounce can tomato paste	1 clove garlic, minced, or ½
3 tablespoons lemon juice	teaspoon garlic powder
¼ cup butter or margarine	pinch of ground red pepper
1 tablespoon chili powder	

1. Combine all ingredients in a small saucepan and mix well. Cook over moderate heat until butter is melted. Cool slightly.

2. Pour sauce over chicken, cover, refrigerate and allow to marinate at least 4 hours.

Yield: 2 cups (enough for two 2½-pound frying chickens)

APRICOT RIBS

4 pounds spareribs	⅓ cup white vinegar
¼ cup apricot brandy, or ½ teaspoon imitation brandy flavoring plus ¼ cup water	2 tablespoons soy sauce
	½ cup brown sugar, packed
	1 clove garlic, minced
one 4-ounce jar strained apricots (baby food)	½ teaspoon finely chopped fresh ginger, or 1 teaspoon ground ginger

1. Cut ribs into serving-size pieces, place in a large pot, cover with water and bring to a boil. Simmer until tender, about 40 minutes. Drain and place in a shallow dish.

2. Combine remaining ingredients and pour over the spareribs. Allow to marinate overnight in the refrigerator. Drain well and reserve the marinade for basting during grilling.

3. Grill over hot coals 40 to 50 minutes, basting frequently.

Serves 4 to 6

IRENE'S VANILLA ICE CREAM

This wonderfully rich homemade ice cream is the perfect base for all kinds of sauces and toppings.

8	eggs, separated	3	cups whipping cream
1⅓	cups sugar	4	cups milk
1	cup light corn syrup	2	tablespoons vanilla

1. In a very large bowl, beat the egg whites until stiff but not dry.

2. In a separate bowl, beat the egg yolks until light, then fold into the beaten whites.

3. Using the electric mixer, beat in the sugar, then the syrup.

4. In another bowl, beat cream with clean beaters until it is thick.

5. Add beaten cream, milk and vanilla to egg mixture and mix well.

6. Cover and refrigerate up to a day before packing into hand or electric ice cream freezer. Follow manufacturer's directions for your freezer.

Yield: 1 gallon

PICNIC NOTE: Transport prepared ice cream mixture in a pre-chilled, wide-mouthed thermal container.

CARROT APPLE CAKE

2	medium-size apples, peeled, cored and finely grated	1	teaspoon baking powder
		1	tablespoon vanilla
3	large carrots, washed and finely grated	1	teaspoon nutmeg
		1	teaspoon cinnamon
1	tablespoon lemon juice	½	teaspoon salt
4	eggs	½	cup milk
1	pound brown sugar	3	cups flour
1½	cups salad oil	½	cup chopped walnuts
grated rind of 1 lemon		½	cup golden raisins
1	teaspoon baking soda	Lemon Cream Frosting (page 83)	

1. Preheat oven to 350°F.

2. Sprinkle apples and carrots with lemon juice. This mixture should measure 2 to 2½ cups, firmly packed. Add more apple or carrot if necessary. Set aside.

3. In a large mixing bowl, beat eggs well. Add sugar, oil, lemon rind and apple-carrot mixture. Blend well, then stir in baking soda, baking powder, vanilla, nutmeg, cinnamon, salt and milk.

4. Stir in half the flour and blend well.

5. Stir in walnuts and raisins, then blend in remaining flour.

6. Spoon batter into well-greased and floured 10-inch tube pan. Bake for 1½ hours or until toothpick inserted in center comes out clean. Allow cake to cool in pan 10 minutes, then invert on plate.

7. When cool, frost with Lemon Cream Frosting.

Serves 12

PICNIC NOTE: This is a dense, moist cake that travels well. It should be refrigerated if kept for a long period of time, but it's so good it will probably disappear before your eyes.

LEMON CREAM FROSTING

4 tablespoons butter or margarine	⅛ teaspoon salt
4 ounces cream cheese at room temperature	1 teaspoon lemon extract
	1 teaspoon grated lemon rind
	1¾ cups confectioners' sugar

1. Cream butter and cream cheese together until fluffy.

2. Add remaining ingredients and mix together until smooth. Add more confectioners' sugar if frosting is too moist to spread smoothly.

3. Spread over top and sides of cake.

Yield: about 2 cups

SANGAREE PUNCH

This colorful punch is only too appropriate for a patriotic picnic feast since Madeira was a favorite imbibement of our Founding Fathers, particularly one Benjamin Franklin.

1½ cups Madeira wine
6 tablespoons lemon juice
6 cups orange juice
sugar to taste
lemon or orange slices

1. Combine all ingredients except lemon or orange slices in a 2-quart container and chill.

2. Pour into ice-filled glasses and garnish with lemon or orange slices.

Serves 6

Bastille Day Picnic Brunch

On July 14th, patriotic French celebrate their national holiday with the same enthusiasm that we do our July 4th Independence Day. Join in the celebration with a Bastille Day picnic brunch spread by a mountain stream or in a field of summer wildflowers. Omelet Breakfast Rolls, hot or cold, form the basis of the meal, complemented by fresh fruit floating in a sparkling beverage, a tangy Broccoli Vinaigrette, and thick slices of eggplant stuffed with meat and rice. End the meal with a nap in the sun after chocolate mousse, a creamy French chocolate delight!

FRUIT TINGLER

This is one of the simplest appetizers or desserts for a hot summer day and it's *so* refreshing. The amount of fruit needed will vary depending on the number of picnickers and the size of the glasses you choose to use. Vary the fruit based on availability.

fresh strawberries, hulled and halved	raisins
melon balls (cantaloupe, watermelon, honeydew)	fresh peaches, peeled, pitted and sliced
green grapes, halved and seeded	chilled lemon-lime soda, champagne or sparkling white wine
	fresh mint sprigs

1. Choose any combination of the fresh fruits listed above and spoon into tall glasses or goblets.

2. Pour soda over all. Garnish with mint sprigs.

3. Serve as a dessert or appetizer.

PICNIC NOTE: Prepare fruits and carry to picnic in individual airtight plastic containers. Place in picnic cooler with chilled soda or wine.

OMELET BREAKFAST ROLLS

But not for breakfast only. These sandwiches are good hot or cold.

6	round hard rolls	6	eggs
3	tablespoons butter or margarine	½	teaspoon salt
		¼	teaspoon pepper
¼	pound fresh mushrooms, sliced	6	slices bacon, crisply fried, drained and crumbled
1	small onion, finely chopped	6	slices cooked ham
1	small green pepper, seeded and finely chopped	6	slices tomato
		6	slices Swiss or Muenster cheese

1. Slice rolls in half crosswise making the bottom half larger than the top. Hollow out the bottom half by removing the soft bread. Reserve interior bread for some other purpose. Set rolls aside.

2. Melt butter in a heavy skillet. Add mushrooms, onion and green pepper, and sauté quickly. Reduce heat to medium-low.

3. Beat eggs with salt and pepper, then add to sautéed vegetables. Add crumbled bacon. Cook until eggs are softly scrambled.

4. Spoon egg mixture into the bottom of each roll. Top with a slice each of ham, tomato and cheese, in that order.

5. Place stuffed rolls under the broiler just long enough to melt the cheese. Cover with roll top and serve immediately.

Serves 6

PICNIC NOTE: If you're preparing these at home to carry to the picnic, assemble sandwiches as directed but omit the grilling under the broiler. Just add roll top, wrap each filled roll in aluminum foil and heat for 15 to 20 minutes at 375°F. Pack rolls close together in a hard-sided container and they will stay warm until serving time provided the distance traveled is not too far. Or you could pack the rolls in a wide-mouthed thermal container.

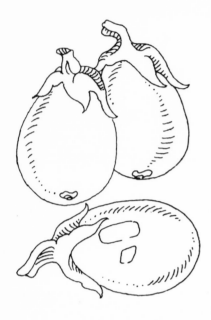

MEAT-STUFFED EGGPLANT

1 large eggplant	1½ cups cold water
4 to 6 tablespoons olive oil	¼ cup slivered almonds
1 medium-size onion, chopped	1 pound lean ground meat
1 clove garlic, minced	½ teaspoon salt
1 tablespoon chopped fresh parsley, or 1½ teaspoons parsley flakes	¼ teaspoon pepper
	¼ cup grated Parmesan cheese
½ cup raw rice	fresh parsley sprigs

1. Boil whole eggplant for 20 minutes. Remove from water, allow to cool, then cut off stem end to make a hole in the top at least 3 inches in diameter.

2. Carefully remove eggplant pulp with a knife and spoon, leaving a shell ½ inch thick. Chop pulp and reserve.

3. In a heavy skillet over low heat, heat oil and sauté onion, garlic and parsley for 4 minutes, then add rice and sauté until it is pale gold.

4. Add cold water to onion-rice mixture. Bring to a boil, then reduce heat and simmer, covered, for 20 minutes. Stir in almonds and remove mixture to medium-size bowl.

5. Preheat oven to 350°F.

6. Brown meat in skillet, then add to rice mixture in bowl.

7. Add more olive oil to skillet, if necessary, and sauté reserved eggplant pulp, seasoned with salt and pepper, until tender. Add meat-rice mixture, mix gently, cover and cook an additional 5 minutes.

8. Using a slotted spoon to drain excess oil, place some of the meat filling inside the eggplant and sprinkle with a little cheese. Press into bottom of eggplant carefully. Continue to layer filling and cheese in the same manner, being sure to fill the eggplant completely and firmly.

9. When eggplant is full, replace the stem end and place vegetable upright in a deep pan. Bake for 15 to 20 minutes. Remove from oven and allow to cool to room temperature. Chill.

10. To serve, slice crosswise. Garnish with fresh parsley sprigs.

Serves 4 to 6

NOTE: Place any leftover filling mixture in a small buttered dish and bake for another meal.

PICNIC NOTE: To pack, put eggplant in a deep box or hard-sided container to avoid crushing. Be sure to pack a sharp knife for slicing along with serving plate and a dessert server or other wide-bladed serving utensil.

BROCCOLI VINAIGRETTE

1 large head broccoli (about 3 pounds)	1 tablespoon Dijon-style mustard, or 1 teaspoon dry mustard
½ cup wine vinegar or tarragon vinegar	1 teaspoon salt
1 tablespoon finely minced shallot	¼ teaspoon white pepper
	½ teaspoon sugar
2 tablespoons finely minced fresh parsley, or 1 teaspoon parsley flakes	1 tablespoon capers, finely chopped
	⅔ cup olive oil

1. Remove large leaves and tough part of the broccoli stalks, and discard. Cut gashes in the bottom of the remaining stalks, then place the head upright in a large saucepan.

2. Pour in boiling water to a depth of about 1½ inches. Cover and steam 12 to 15 minutes, until just fork tender. Remove from pan, allow to cool, then break apart into 6 to 8 servings and arrange on a platter. Cover with transparent wrap and chill.

3. Combine remaining ingredients except oil in a small bowl and beat vigorously to mix. Add oil slowly while beating with a wire whisk or rotary beater to make a creamy sauce. Pour into a small jar and refrigerate.

4. To serve, arrange broccoli on a serving platter or in individual salad bowls and spoon on vinaigrette sauce. Serve immediately.

Serves 6 to 8

Variations: Steamed asparagus spears can be substituted for the broccoli if you prefer. Or try mixing steamed cauliflower flowerets with the broccoli.

DOUBLE CHOCOLATE MOUSSE

1 cup semisweet chocolate pieces	1 tablespoon Kahlua liqueur or coffee brandy (optional)
¼ cup sweet butter	
1 teaspoon vanilla	4 eggs, separated
2 teaspoons instant coffee	¾ cup sugar
¼ cup boiling water	whole almonds

1. Whirl chocolate in blender until powdery. Add butter and vanilla, instant coffee, boiling water and Kahlua (if desired), and blend until smooth.

2. Beat the egg yolks with the sugar until the mixture is thick and falls back on itself in a ribbon. Add to whirling chocolate mixture and blend thoroughly.

3. In a large clean bowl, beat the egg whites until they hold stiff, distinct short peaks. Pour chocolate mixture into the whites and fold until well blended.

4. Pour into parfait glasses or small pots and cover lightly with transparent wrap. Refrigerate at least 1 hour before serving.

5. Garnish with whole almonds.

Serves 6

PICNIC NOTE: Use pretty paper muffin cups in muffin tins in place of glasses or pots for an easy way to transport this dessert. *Due to the raw egg content, this dessert must be kept thoroughly chilled prior to serving.* Do not allow it to sit out in the hot sun.

FRESH MINT TEA

12 lumps of sugar	2 quarts strong hot tea
1 quart fresh mint sprigs, washed	

1. Place 2 lumps of sugar in each large cup or mug.

2. Fill each cup loosely with whole fresh mint sprigs.

3. Pour hot tea over the mint. Stir carefully to dissolve the sugar.

PICNIC NOTE: If mint grows wildly and profusely at one of your favorite summer picnic sites, be sure to include this delicious drink in the menu. If you prefer, it can be brewed in a large container, then served over ice.

Captain's Table Picnic

Dinner at the captain's table is a fitting way to end a day of boating. Tie up at the dock to enjoy a hearty picnic supper that you can carry on board in a picnic cooler.

If your boat is large enough, you could consider cooking the filet on a small hibachi or barbecue grill fitted with an ash catcher to avoid flying sparks. Serve the steak hot on thick slices of French bread. Or take along the makings for Shish Kebab (page 209), and let each member of the crew assemble his or her own. A rich dessert like Coffee Brandy Walnut Pie is bound to please even the hungriest of sailors.

MENU

Shrimp Seviche*

Iced Zucchini Soup*

Cold Sliced Filet Mignon

Cucumber-Horseradish Sauce*

Picnic Eggs*

French Bread

Mushroom-Stuffed Tomato Shells*

Fresh Fruit

Coffee Brandy Walnut Pie*

Coffee

SHRIMP SEVICHE

This spicy fish appetizer, normally made with raw fish, is a favorite South American appetizer. This version will appeal to those who can't bear the thought of raw fish and it can be served as an appetizer or salad course. For those who do appreciate raw fish, substitute 2 pounds of flounder and ¼ pound raw scallops, both cut into slivers, for the shrimp. Also substitute lime juice for the lemon and orange juice.

2 pounds fresh shrimp, cooked, shelled and cleaned
½ cup fresh lemon juice
½ cup fresh orange juice
6 tablespoons finely diced red onion
½ cup chopped fresh parsley
1 small tomato, peeled, seeded and cut into strips
2 green chili peppers, finely chopped

1 clove garlic, minced
1 teaspoon salt
1 teaspoon freshly ground pepper
1 teaspoon crushed coriander seed
dash of Tabasco sauce
½ cup olive oil
6 medium-size green peppers, seeded

1. Cut shrimp into small pieces and cover with lemon and orange juice. Cover and marinate 1 hour at room temperature.

2. Add onion, parsley, tomato, chili peppers, garlic and seasonings, and mix well.

3. Add oil and toss gently. Chill at least 1 hour.

4. Fill green pepper shells with Seviche lifted from marinade with slotted spoon.

Serves 6

ICED ZUCCHINI SOUP

1 pound zucchini, cubed (about 3 medium-size)
1 medium-size onion, coarsely chopped
2 scallions, coarsely chopped (including part of green tops)
1 stalk celery, coarsely chopped
5 sprigs fresh parsley
2 sprigs fresh basil, or 1 teaspoon dried basil
3 cups chicken broth
salt and pepper to taste
1 cup light cream
2 egg yolks
fresh parsley

1. Combine all but the last three ingredients in a large saucepan and bring to a boil. Reduce heat to medium and simmer, uncovered, 40 to 50 minutes.

2. Pour half of cooked mixture into the blender jar, cover tightly and purée. Transfer to a large bowl. Repeat with the remaining mixture.

3. Beat cream and egg yolks together until well blended. Add to purée and mix well. Cover and refrigerate to chill.

4. Stir well before serving and garnish with fresh parsley.

Yield: 5 to 6 cups

PICNIC NOTE: Due to raw egg content, this soup must be kept thoroughly chilled until serving time.

CUCUMBER-HORSERADISH SAUCE

1 cup dairy sour cream
1 small cucumber, finely diced
1 tablespoon prepared horseradish (or more, to your liking)
⅛ teaspoon salt

1. Mix all ingredients together in a small bowl.

2. Serve with cold sliced filet mignon.

Yield: 1 cup

PICNIC EGGS

8 hard-cooked eggs, cooled and peeled
⅓ to ½ cup Mayonnaise (page 190)
1 tablespoon Dijon-style mustard
¼ cup finely chopped cooked ham
1 teaspoon finely chopped fresh parsley
grated rind of 1 lemon (*do not omit*)

1 tablespoon fresh lemon juice
1 shallot, finely minced
salt and pepper to taste
⅛ teaspoon garlic powder
⅛ teaspoon celery salt
4 teaspoons sugar
pepper or paprika
1 to 2 tablespoons grated Swiss or Cheddar cheese (optional)
fresh parsley or dill sprigs

1. Cut eggs in half lengthwise and carefully remove the yolks to a small bowl. Reserve 1 yolk for use as a salad garnish.

2. Mash yolks well or whirl in a blender. Add Mayonnaise and mustard, and mix to a smooth paste.

3. Add remaining ingredients except cheese and parsley or dill, and mix well. Mixture should be spreadable but not runny. Add 1 to 2 tablespoons grated Swiss or Cheddar cheese if mixture is too runny.

4. Fill each egg half with a scoop of the mixture and dust each with pepper or paprika. Garnish with fresh parsley or dill.

Serves 8

PICNIC NOTE: These require refrigerated storage. For pretty packing assemble stuffed egg halves in pairs, yolk to yolk, and wrap in transparent wrap, then in squares of brightly colored tissue paper twisted at both ends. Layer in a hard-sided airtight container and place in picnic cooler.

MUSHROOM-STUFFED TOMATO SHELLS

6 medium- to large-size tomatoes	1 recipe Marinated Mushrooms (below)
salt	6 sprigs fresh parsley

1. Wash tomatoes and remove top stems. Slice off ¼ to ½ inch of tops and set tops aside.

2. Carefully remove the pulp and seeds, and reserve for use in a soup or sauce.

3. Salt tomato shells and tops and set shells upside down to drain on a plate covered with a double layer of paper towels. Place fleshy sides of tops on paper towels. Allow to drain for at least 30 minutes.

4. Fill shells with Marinated Mushrooms.

5. Pull 1 full sprig of parsley through the hole in each tomato top and snip excess stem. Use to cover stuffed shells. Refrigerate until 30 minutes before serving time.

Serves 6

Variations: Tomato Shells prepared in the manner described above can be filled with a variety of vegetable, fish or meat mixtures for countless variations of a colorful addition to any picnic meal.

MARINATED MUSHROOMS

1 pound fresh mushrooms	½ teaspoon dried thyme
½ cup olive oil	1 teaspoon dried basil
1 clove garlic, minced	1 teaspoon sugar
¼ cup lemon juice	3 peppercorns
1 tablespoon white wine vinegar	6 scallions, coarsely chopped (including part of the green tops)
salt	
1 bay leaf	
1 full sprig fresh parsley, minced	

1. Wipe mushrooms clean with a damp cloth and trim the stem ends. Cut mushrooms in half lengthwise. Quarter large ones.

2. Heat oil in a large heavy skillet. Add all ingredients except scallions to the hot oil and simmer 5 minutes, no longer. Remove from heat and set aside to cool.

3. Pour mushrooms and cooking juices into a glass or earthenware bowl and add the scallions. Toss to mix.

4. To use as a filling for Tomato Shells, lift mushrooms from the liquid with a slotted spoon.

Serves 6

COFFEE BRANDY WALNUT PIE

1 recipe Single Crust
    Pastry (page 188)
1 cup walnut halves
¼ cup coffee brandy
1 cup brown sugar, packed
2 tablespoons all-purpose
    flour

1 tablespoon butter or
    margarine, softened
1 cup dark corn syrup
3 eggs, beaten
¼ teaspoon salt
whipped cream (optional)
instant coffee (optional)

1. Preheat oven to 325°F.

2. Prepare pastry according to directions on page 188. Roll out to a 12-inch circle on a lightly floured surface. Fit into a 9-inch pie plate. Trim overhang and turn under and flute edges. Set aside.

3. Toss walnuts with brandy and let stand 1 hour.

4. Combine brown sugar and flour and beat in the butter until creamy. Beat in corn syrup, eggs and salt. Stir in the walnuts and brandy.

5. Spread mixture in prepared pastry shell. Cover the edge of the pastry with a narrow strip of foil to prevent burning. Remove during the last 15 minutes of baking. Bake for 1 hour and 10 minutes or until the center is set.

6. Serve with whipped cream sprinkled with instant coffee granules if desired.

Serves 6 to 8

Italian Beach Blanket Lunch

Italian antipasto, a wide array of fish, meat, cheese and crunchy vegetables attractively arranged on a large platter, is all sun worshippers really need to satisfy their sea-air hunger. The chilled meat and vegetable platter will stay fresh in the top of an insulated picnic cooler packed with plenty of ice and club soda for wine spritzers, so refreshing on hot summer beach days. Fresh fruit is a must for day-long munching with cheese and complements a tart, rich cake sure to please any beachcomber's sweet tooth, Italian or otherwise!

BEACH BLANKET ANTIPASTO

2 small heads butter or Boston lettuce, washed and drained	1 pound thinly sliced Provolone cheese
one 10¾-ounce can water-packed tuna fish	2 medium-size cucumbers, sliced
6 large celery stalks	2 to 3 large carrots, shredded and tossed with a little lemon juice
4 hard-cooked eggs, cooled, peeled and sliced	one 3-ounce can sardines
1 pound thinly sliced dry salami	one 2-ounce can anchovies

Dressing

½ cup olive oil	¼ teaspoon dried basil
½ cup red wine vinegar	¼ teaspoon dried oregano
¼ teaspoon salt	1 clove garlic, minced
dash of pepper	

1. Line a very large, shallow salad bowl (or large pizza plate) with lettuce leaves. Pack remaining leaves in airtight container.

2. Drain tuna fish and turn out onto the center of the lettuce-lined bowl.

3. Thoroughly clean and trim celery stalks and arrange, spoke-fashion, on lettuce.

4. Arrange sliced eggs, salami, cheese, cucumbers, shredded carrots, and sardines and anchovies, each in a separate section formed by the celery.

5. Wrap bowl in heavy-duty aluminum foil and chill several hours.

6. To make dressing, combine ingredients in a shaker jar and shake vigorously to mix.

†Prepare Lemon-Herbed Summer Vegetables as directed on page 115, omitting the pineapple.

7. To serve, unwrap antipasto bowl and surround with dressing, freshly grated Parmesan cheese, thinly sliced Italian bread, a crock of sweet butter and small bowls of Orange Marinated Onions, Greek Artichoke Salad and Lemon-Herbed Summer Vegetables. Allow each picnicker to compose his own salad or sandwich with the ingredients provided.

Serves 6

GREEK ARTICHOKE SALAD

two	15-ounce cans arti-choke hearts, drained	½	teaspoon dried basil
⅓	cup olive oil	⅛	teaspoon pepper
2	tablespoons lemon juice	¼	pound Feta cheese, crumbled
2	tablespoons white wine vinegar	¼	pound Greek olives, drained
1	clove garlic, minced		butter lettuce
1	teaspoon dried tarragon		

1. Place artichokes in medium-size bowl.

2. Place oil, lemon juice, vinegar, garlic, tarragon, basil and pepper in a shaker jar and shake vigorously to mix well. Transfer dressing to a small saucepan and heat to simmering over a medium heat.

3. Pour at once over artichokes and allow to marinate at room temperature 1 to 3 hours. Cover and chill until ready to serve. This salad is best when allowed to marinate several days.

4. At serving time, add cheese and olives and toss gently. To serve, lift vegetables from marinade and place on leaves of butter lettuce.

Serves 6 to 8

PICNIC NOTE: Before packing, toss the artichokes with the cheese and olives and carry the mix to the picnic in a covered container. Wash the lettuce in ice water, break it into leaves and wrap it carefully in paper towels. Carry to the picnic in a cooler.

LEMON LEMON DRIZZLE CAKE

Drenched in lemon, this cake is sure to rate rave reviews whenever you serve it!

¾ cup butter or margarine	1½ teaspoons baking powder
1 cup sugar	¼ teaspoon salt
one 3-ounce package lemon-flavored gelatin	½ cup milk
	¾ cup confectioners' sugar
¼ cup dairy sour cream	2 tablespoons freshly squeezed lemon juice
4 eggs	
2 cups all-purpose flour	2 teaspoons grated lemon rind

1. Preheat oven to 375°F.

2. Cream butter and sugar together until light and fluffy. Add gelatin and sour cream and mix well.

3. Add eggs, one at a time, beating well after each addition.

4. Combine flour, baking powder and salt, and add to creamed mixture alternately with milk.

5. Turn batter into a well-greased and floured 9-inch square baking pan and bake for 30 minutes. Reduce heat to 350°F and continue to bake until toothpick inserted in center comes out clean, about 15 to 20 minutes.

6. Mix remaining ingredients in a small bowl until smooth.

7. Prick the top of the baked cake all over with a toothpick. Drizzle lemon-sugar mixture over the hot cake. Allow to cool, then cut in squares.

Serves 9

Variation: Substitute orange gelatin, orange juice and orange rind for the lemon ingredients.

Sweet-Sour Asparagus with Walnuts (page 48) and Shrimp in Lemon Cups (page 49)

Moving Day Picnic (page 58)

Chocolate Pecan Pie (page 71)

Italian Beach Blanket Lunch (page 94)

Cheese and Spinach Pie (page 156) and Greek Cookies (page 160)

Halloween Afternoon Outing (page 135)

Picnic on Ice (page 170)

Christmas Picnic Package (page 175)

Picnic Salad Bar

Try this picnic on a hot summer afternoon when you don't feel like cooking and all your favorite vegetables are in season and abundant at your local farmers' market. Choose any or all of the ingredients listed in the Salad Bar charts to lay out a colorful buffet on the picnic cloth. Picnickers choose from your offerings to devise their own special salads and then top them off with one of several special dressings. Be sure to provide sturdy paper picnic bowls or your own bright plastic salad bowls.

Crusty pizza-flavored bread complements any salad a picnicker concocts. If you make it ahead of time, then freeze it for a hot day, you'll only need to heat it in the oven after thawing unless you prefer it at room temperature.

The cold soup that starts the meal and the fruit tarts for dessert are so simple to make they'll probably become standby favorites for summer entertaining on short notice.

LAST MINUTE APRICOT SOUP

This soup is a tasty alternative to fruit soups that simmer an hour to soften the fruits before puréeing, thus heating up the kitchen on a hot day. A refreshing starter for any summer picnic meal, this soup can be prepared at a moment's notice.

one 16-ounce can apricot halves (including canning syrup)	1 cup fruit juice (orange, apple, cranberry or apricot)
one 16-ounce can peach halves or slices (including canning syrup)	sour cream (optional) sliced dried apricots (optional)

1. Purée canned apricots and peaches in a blender.

2. Add fruit juice and sour cream and blend well. Chill.

3. Serve with dried apricot slices and a dollop of sour cream on top if desired.

Yield: about 6 cups

Variations: You can make countless versions of this fruit soup by mixing and matching two 16-ounce cans of your favorite canned fruits and varying the fruit juice you use. Try yogurt as an alternative to the sour cream if you prefer. Also try adding ½ to 2 teaspoons of spices like cinnamon, allspice and nutmeg. A combination of peaches, cherries and cranberry juice is just one of the countless possible variations.

SALAD BAR

Since each picnicker is left to his or her own devices, there is no formal recipe for a salad bar. Instead, use the following chart as a guide in choosing offerings. Ingredients are bound to vary depending on the time of the year and the locale.

SALAD INGREDIENTS

Greens: Washed, drained, torn into bite-size pieces plus enough large unbroken leaves to line a large salad bowl; choose several of the following.

iceberg lettuce	escarole	spinach	Boston lettuce	watercress	romaine

Crunch and Color: Choose several from each list for lots of variety in color and texture.

red and yellow	green	white
red cabbage, shredded	scallions with tops, chopped	bean sprouts
raw red beets, shredded	raw broccoli flowerets	white cabbage, shredded
canned shoestring beets, drained	green pepper rings	raw cauliflower flowerets
purple onions, sliced	celery, sliced	raw mushrooms, sliced at picnic site
red radishes, sliced	marinated artichoke hearts (purchased)	marinated mushrooms (page 92)
cherry tomatoes, stemmed	raw green beans	chick peas, drained
tomato wedges	zucchini with skin, sliced	cucumber, peeled and sliced
carrots, sliced	avocado, peeled, pitted and sliced at picnic	
summer squash, sliced		
kidney beans, drained		

A Little Substance: Meat, seafood and cheese.

meat (cut into narrow strips)	seafood	cheese
boiled ham	tuna fish, flaked	Cheddar, shredded
roast turkey or chicken breast	salmon, boned and flaked	Swiss or Jarlsberg in strips or chunks
roast beef	smoked oysters, drained	blue, crumbled
salami	tiny shrimp, drained	Feta, crumbled
	chunks of boiled lobster	cottage cheese

Toppers: Add a little zest.

bacon, crisply fried and crumbled
french-fried onion rings
hard-cooked egg, chopped
Parmesan cheese, grated
croutons
grated lemon rind
sunflower or pumpkin seeds
chopped walnuts, pecans or almonds
raisins or chopped dates
wheat germ

General Directions for Salad Bar

1. Line a large salad bowl with lettuce leaves and fill with a mixture of the chosen greens torn into bite-size pieces. Pack on ice in picnic cooler or basket (see page 13).

2. Prepare as many of the remaining vegetables and other ingredients as desired and pack in airtight plastic containers or plastic bags, carefully sealed. Place in cooler until serving time.

3. At the picnic site, place salad ingredients in small individual bowls and arrange around greens-filled bowl. Provide a serving spoon or tongs for each ingredient.

4. Serve with a choice of salad dressings.

AVOCADO DRESSING

¼ teaspoon coriander seed
1 small ripe avocado, peeled, pitted and sliced
2 teaspoons minced onion
2 tablespoons lime juice
½ cup dairy sour cream
⅛ teaspoon hot sauce (or more, to your liking)
⅛ teaspoon garlic powder
salt and pepper to taste

1. Whirl coriander seeds in blender to pulverize.

2. Add avocado, onion and lime juice. Purée to a smooth paste.

3. Fold in sour cream and seasonings. Taste and adjust seasonings to your liking.

Yield: 1 cup

COTTAGE CHEESE DRESSING

1 tablespoon white vinegar
1 teaspoon prepared mustard
1 tablespoon lemon juice
6 tablespoons olive oil
¼ cup minced onion
¼ cup small curd cottage cheese
salt and pepper to taste
6 slices bacon, crisply fried, drained and crumbled

1. Place all ingredients except bacon in a shaker jar and shake vigorously to mix well. Refrigerate overnight.

2. Just before serving, add crumbled bacon to dressing and shake to mix.

Yield: ¾ cup

PINE NUT DRESSING

⅔ cup pine nuts	½ teaspoon grated lemon peel
6 tablespoons olive oil	½ teaspoon dried tarragon
3 tablespoons wine vinegar	½ teaspoon salt
⅛ teaspoon nutmeg	

1. Preheat oven to 350°F.

2. Spread pine nuts in a single layer in a shallow pan. Bake for 5 to 8 minutes, until golden. Stir occasionally. Remove from oven and allow to cool.

3. Place remaining ingredients in a shaker jar with the pine nuts and mix well. Let stand at room temperature at least 1 hour, or as long as overnight.

Yield: about ¾ cup

PIZZA PICNIC LOAF

one 1-pound loaf frozen bread dough	½ teaspoon salt
	dash of pepper
3 tablespoons butter or margarine	½ cup snipped fresh parsley (preferably Italian)
1 small onion, finely chopped	olive oil
1 clove garlic, finely minced	¾ cup small curd cottage cheese
one 15-ounce can tomato sauce	
1 bay leaf	one 6-ounce can sliced mushrooms, drained
¼ teaspoon dried oregano	¾ cup shredded mozzarella cheese
½ teaspoon dried basil	

1. Remove loaf of dough from package and thaw as package directs until dough is pliable, about 1 to 2 hours.

2. Melt butter in a heavy skillet and sauté onion and garlic until the onion is transparent. Stir in tomato sauce, bay leaf, oregano, basil, salt and pepper. Simmer over low heat about 45 minutes. Remove bay leaf. Stir in parsley, then adjust seasonings. Set mixture aside.

3. On a lightly floured surface, roll out bread dough to a 16 × 12-inch rectangle. Brush surface with oil.

4. Stir cottage cheese into tomato sauce. Spread evenly over surface of dough. Sprinkle mushrooms over tomato sauce, then sprinkle cheese on top.

5. Carefully fold dough lengthwise so edges meet in the middle.

Pinch to seal seam and turn ends under to seal. Place loaf, seam side down, on a greased baking sheet. Cover and let rise in a warm place until double, about 1 hour.

6. Preheat oven to 350°F.

7. Brush loaf with oil and pierce with fork to create steam vents. Bake for 1 hour or until loaf sounds hollow when tapped. Cool to room temperature.

8. Serve thickly sliced at room temperature or cold.

Yield: ten ¾-inch slices

Variations: For an even easier version, substitute your favorite commercial tomato sauce for the homemade. You'll need about ¾ cup of sauce. You can spread the sauce-covered dough with any of your favorite pizza toppings—chopped green pepper, anchovies, browned ground meat, pepperoni—before folding and setting the loaf to rise.

TINY FRUIT TARTS

fresh raspberries,
    strawberries or green
    grapes
purchased graham cracker-
    lined tart pans

currant jelly
whipped or dairy sour cream

1. Wash and hull fruit as necessary.

2. Pile fruit in tart pans.

3. Heat currant jelly in a small saucepan until melted and pour it over fruit to glaze.

4. Serve with a dollop of whipped or sour cream from the cooler.

Tropical Luau Lunch

This version of the traditional Hawaiian feast centers around a ham baked in a brandied cranberry sauce. You can bake the ham completely in the oven at home, or finish cooking it on the grill at the picnic site. You can also serve the marinated vegetables as a salad, or skewer them and grill them over the coals while you finish the ham.

While the meat and vegetables grill, treat picnic guests to a Puu Puu Tray, a platter of tasty appetizers with special dipping sauces. Use palm leaf fans from your local import shop for place mats to add to the tropical atmosphere. Fresh pineapple, a symbol of hospitality in America since colonial times, provides dessert—mounds of fresh fruit heaped in hollowed-out pineapple halves and marinated in fresh orange juice.

CURRIED CHICKEN BITS

2 large whole chicken breasts
1 tablespoon peanut or vegetable oil
1 tablespoon water
1 egg, beaten
¾ cup all-purpose flour
1½ teaspoons curry powder (or more, to your liking)
¼ teaspoon ground ginger
dash of salt and pepper
pinch of monosodium glutamate (optional)
¼ to ½ cup butter (don't substitute margarine or cooking oil)
Mustard Sauce (page 111)

1. Skin and bone chicken breasts and cut into small pieces no larger than your thumb.

2. Combine oil, water and beaten egg, and add chicken pieces. Refrigerate and allow to marinate for 1 hour.

3. In a small brown paper bag, combine flour, curry powder, ginger, salt, pepper and monosodium glutamate (if desired), and shake to mix well.

4. Lift chicken bits from the marinade and add to the flour mixture in the paper bag. Shake until bits are well coated.

5. Melt butter in a heavy skillet or wok. Sauté the floured chicken bits until golden brown. Drain on paper towels.

6. Serve hot or chilled with Mustard Sauce.

Serves 6

MUSTARD SAUCE

½ cup red wine
¼ cup prepared mustard
¼ teaspoon pepper
½ teaspoon salt

1 scallion, finely chopped
   (including part of the
   green top)
¼ teaspoon curry powder

1. Combine all ingredients in a small saucepan and bring to a boil. Reduce heat and simmer for 5 minutes, stirring frequently.

2. Serve in small dishes as a dipping sauce for Curried Chicken Bits.

Yield: about ¾ cup

SALMON-STUFFED CHERRY TOMATOES

24 to 30 large cherry tomatoes
one 8-ounce package cream
     cheese
1 tablespoon Dijon-style
   mustard
1 teaspoon lemon juice
one 10-ounce can salmon

1 tablespoon finely
   chopped onion
½ teaspoon dried dill
½ teaspoon grated lemon rind
salt and pepper to taste
fresh parsley or dill sprigs

1. Cut a thin slice from the top of each cherry tomato and carefully remove pulp and seeds. Set tomato shells aside and refrigerate pulp for some other use.

2. Soften cream cheese with mustard and lemon juice, and beat until fluffy.

3. Drain salmon, then break it into fine flakes and remove bones. Add to cream cheese mixture.

4. Add remaining ingredients except parsley or dill sprigs and beat well.

5. Fill cherry tomato shells with salmon mixture and garnish each with a small sprig of fresh parsley or dill. Chill.

Yield: 24 to 30 appetizers

Variation:

SALMON BUTTER BALL

1. Follow Steps 2 through 4, above, substituting ½ cup butter for the cream cheese.

2. Pack the salmon butter in a small tub or crock, cover and refrigerate until firm. Roll into a ball, wrap in waxed paper and rechill.

3. Serve as a cocktail ball with crackers or Melba toast.

SPICY MEATBALLS

2   slices dry white bread,
        torn into small pieces
2   eggs, beaten
1½   pounds ground lamb or
        beef
½   cup raisins
¼   cup chopped onions
1-inch piece fresh ginger,
        peeled and finely chopped
¼   teaspoon ground cloves
1   teaspoon salt
¼   teaspoon pepper
2   teaspoons dried mint
dash of cayenne
6   tablespoons vegetable oil
Curried Yogurt (below)

1. Soak bread in beaten eggs. Add remaining ingredients except oil and yogurt, and knead together until well mixed. Shape into walnut-size balls.

2. Heat oil in a large heavy skillet. Fry meatballs over medium heat, turning often, until well browned.

3. Serve hot or cold with Curried Yogurt.

Yield: 24 to 30 appetizers

CURRIED YOGURT
½   medium to large banana
¾   cup plain yogurt
1   teaspoon curry powder
salt and pepper to taste
2   tablespoons dairy sour
        cream

1. Combine banana, yogurt, curry powder, salt and pepper in blender, and whirl until smooth.

2. Fold in sour cream. Cover and refrigerate.

Yield: 1 cup

PICNIC HAM

1 smoked precooked ham (allow ½ to ¾ pound per person)	whole cloves Brandied Cranberry Sauce (below)

1. Preheat oven to 400°F.

2. Score the fatty part of the ham in a diamond design. Decorate each diamond with a whole clove.

3. Bake uncovered for 1 hour. Drain off the grease released by cooking.

4. Pour Brandied Cranberry Sauce over ham and bake an additional 30 minutes, or place ham on the grill over medium coals and continue cooking an additional 1 to 1½ hours, basting frequently with sauce. Interior temperature of ham should be 130°F on a meat thermometer.

5. Slice ham thinly and arrange on a serving platter. Spoon sauce over the top.

PICNIC NOTE: Ham can be transported in the sauce and sliced just before serving. Cover the ham in its baking pan with foil and then wrap in layers of newspaper to keep it warm until serving time.

BRANDIED CRANBERRY SAUCE

¼ cup butter	2 tablespoons honey
one 16-ounce can whole cranberry sauce	½ teaspoon Worcestershire sauce
½ cup apricot or pineapple preserves	½ teaspoon salt
¼ cup prepared mustard	⅛ teaspoon pepper
1 cup brandy, or ½ teaspoon imitation brandy flavoring plus 1 cup water	¼ teaspoon cinnamon
	¼ teaspoon ground cloves
	¼ teaspoon ground ginger

1. Melt butter in a heavy saucepan. Stir in remaining ingredients and mix well. Simmer 30 minutes.

2. Pour over smoked ham while baking or brush over meats and vegetables during the last 20 minutes of barbecuing.

3. This sauce can be used hot or chilled.

Yield: about 4 cups

DATE-STUFFED SWEET POTATOES

6 medium-size sweet potatoes	3 tablespoons butter, melted
1 cup finely chopped dates	½ cup coarsely chopped
2 tablespoons brown sugar	walnuts
orange juice	

1. Boil sweet potatoes in their jackets until just barely tender, about 45 minutes depending on size. Drain and cool until potatoes are easy to handle.

2. Preheat oven to 450°F.

3. Peel potatoes and cut the points off each end. Cut each potato in half crosswise. With an apple corer, carefully remove the center of each potato. Place potatoes on end in a lightly greased baking dish.

4. Combine dates with brown sugar and enough orange juice to moisten. Fill cavities in potatoes with date mixture. Brush potatoes with melted butter and sprinkle with walnuts. Brown in oven about 10 to 15 minutes.

5. Serve hot or cold.

Serves 6

Variations: Substitute rum, coffee brandy, Kahlua or Grand Marnier liqueur for the orange juice.

PICNIC NOTE: Keep this dish warm by wrapping the baking dish in foil, then in layers of newspaper. Or transfer it carefully to a wide-mouthed thermal container.

CRAB AND RICE SALAD

2 cups cooked rice	1 red pepper, seeded and
1 cup olive oil	cut into fine strips
juice of 1 lemon	1 green pepper, seeded and
1 teaspoon grated lemon rind	cut into fine strips
salt and pepper to taste	¼ cup chopped chives
dash of cayenne pepper	6 sweet gherkins, coarsely
1½ cups frozen corn kernels	chopped
1 cup fresh, flaked crabmeat	10 walnuts, sliced

1. Heat rice in the top of a double boiler. Add oil and mix well. Add lemon juice and rind, salt and pepper to taste and cayenne. Allow to cool to room temperature.

2. In a medium-size saucepan, boil corn kernels in salted water for 2 minutes *only*. Transfer to a colander and rinse with ice cold water until corn is well chilled.

3. When rice is cool, add remaining ingredients except walnuts. Toss to mix well. Sprinkle walnuts on top, cover and chill.

Serves 6 to 8

LEMON-HERBED SUMMER VEGETABLES

1   pint basket cherry tomatoes
boiling water
1   recipe Lemon Tarragon
         Dressing (page 116)
½   pound small white
         mushrooms
1½   pounds small zucchini,
         cut into 1-inch slices
1½   cups fresh pineapple
         chunks, or one 8-
         ounce can pineapple
         chunks, drained
lettuce

1. Place the tomatoes, a few at a time, in a small colander and dip the colander into a large pan of rapidly boiling water for 15 seconds. Rinse immediately with ice cold water. Slip off and discard the skins and stems. Place tomatoes in a small bowl with a tight-fitting lid.

2. Pour half of the Lemon Tarragon Dressing over tomatoes. Cover and chill at least 2 hours, stirring carefully several times.

3. Clean mushrooms with a damp cloth and trim stems.

4. Combine mushrooms with zucchini in a small bowl, and pour remaining dressing over them. Cover, refrigerate and allow to marinate at least 2 hours, stirring several times.

5. Remove tomatoes, mushrooms and zucchini from the marinade and toss with pineapple chunks.

6. Serve on a bed of lettuce with some of the dressing spooned over the top.

Serves 6 to 8

Variation: Instead of serving these as a salad, thread marinated vegetables and fresh pineapple chunks on skewers and cook over medium coals, turning occasionally and basting frequently with the dressing.

LEMON TARRAGON DRESSING

one 6-ounce can frozen
     lemonade
     concentrate, thawed
     and undiluted
¾ cup vegetable oil
¼ cup white vinegar

3 tablespoons sugar
¼ teaspoon salt
dash of pepper
½ teaspoon grated lemon rind
½ teaspoon dry mustard
1½ teaspoons dried tarragon

1. Mix ingredients together in shaker jar or blender. Cover and refrigerate.

2. Use as a marinade for vegetables or meats, or serve over mixed greens or fruit salad.

Yield: 1¾ to 2 cups

ISLAND FRUIT BOATS

1 large fresh pineapple
1 large orange, peeled,
   sectioned and chopped
1 pint basket strawberries,
   hulled and sliced
1 medium-size cantaloupe,
   seeded and made into
   melon balls

1 cup halved seedless green
   grapes
½ cup fresh orange juice
juice of 2 limes
shredded coconut
lime slices
1 pint plain yogurt (optional)

1. Slice pineapple in half lengthwise. Remove and discard hard inner core. Carefully scoop out fruit and cut into cubes. Cover pineapple halves with transparent wrap and refrigerate.

2. Combine pineapple cubes with other fruits in a large glass bowl, and toss with orange juice. Add lime juice, cover and refrigerate several hours to marinate.

3. Fill pineapple shells with marinated fruit. Sprinkle with shredded coconut and garnish with lime slices.

4. Serve with plain yogurt if desired.

Serves 8 to 10

PICNIC NOTE: Transport chilled pineapple halves and marinated fruit separately. Fill the "boats" just prior to serving.

LUAU PUNCH

one 6-ounce can frozen grape juice concentrate	2 cups canned crushed pineapple (including canning syrup)
water	2 quarts chilled ginger ale or lemon-lime soda
1 cup orange juice	cucumber slices
1 cup fresh lemon juice	

1. Dilute grape juice concentrate in a gallon container according to package directions.

2. Stir in remaining ingredients except ginger ale. Chill.

3. At serving time, add ginger ale. Serve over ice using a ladle to include some of the pineapple in each serving. Garnish each serving with a slice of cucumber.

Yield: about 1 gallon

COCO LOCO

For each serving:

1 cup cracked ice	2 tablespoons Coconut Cream (below)
2 ounces white rum	1 teaspoon sugar

1. Combine ingredients in blender, and frappé until smooth and foamy.

2. Serve with a straw.

COCONUT CREAM

2 cups cream, heated	1 cup flaked coconut

1. Pour cream over coconut and let stand 30 minutes.

2. Strain through a fine sieve. Chill.

Yield: 2 cups

Hamburger Heaven

No picnic cookbook would be complete without the all-American hamburger. A simple hamburger grilled over hot coals and trimmed with the traditional condiments is sure to please just about anyone, especially the children in the crowd. But hamburgers need not be ordinary, everyday fare at a cookout. With a little imagination and a variety of toppings, picnickers can create taste-tempting variations that would send anyone to "hamburger heaven." Homemade Burger Buns and Pita Bread (page 159) or English muffins are good substitutes for purchased buns and they can all be heated and/or toasted on the grill while the burgers are cooking. The chart of Hamburger Put-Togethers which follows is full of suggestions, but your imagination and that of fellow picnickers is the limit to the possible combinations.

For the best hamburgers, purchase good-quality ground round or ground chuck from your favorite butcher—prepackaged hamburger meat is usually very fatty and shrinks substantially in the cooking process. Don't choose ground sirloin, either. It can be very dry and tasteless. If you must purchase prepackaged meat, be sure it is *lean* ground beef. In preparing hamburger patties, handle the meat as little as possible. The result is tender hamburgers rather than tough ones.

Unless otherwise indicated, prepare hamburger patties for any of the "put-togethers" by seasoning the ground meat with 1 teaspoon salt and ⅛ teaspoon pepper per pound. Shape the meat into patties and place them on the grill over slow coals. It should take approximately 5 minutes per side to cook hamburgers unless they have been stuffed (see page 121). Consider making hamburger patties ahead of time and then stacking them in an empty coffee can with squares of aluminum foil or waxed paper separating the patties. Seal the top with a layer of transparent wrap, a layer of foil and the plastic lid to the can. Freeze. When packing cookout ingredients, remove the can from the freezer and use it as an extra cooling agent in your picnic hamper if you'll be traveling a long distance to the picnic site. If travel time is too short to expect burgers to thaw, move the can from the freezer to the refrigerator to thaw the night before the scheduled outing, then pack it in the picnic cooler.

Recipes for the starred (*) items in the chart which follows are included here or on the pages indicated in parentheses.

HAMBURGER PUT-TOGETHERS

Burger	Bread	Toppings	Sauces	Preparation Notes
Bacon-Avocado	sesame seed burger buns	fried bacon slices tomato slices	Avocado Nut Butter (page 73)	1. Cook bacon on grill while burgers cook. 2. Coat both bun halves liberally with Avocado Butter. 3. Top burger with bacon and tomato.
Breakfast Eye-Opener	English muffin	fried egg Golden Onions*	paprika ketchup	1. Toast muffin on buttered grill. 2. After turning burgers to cook the second side, fry eggs in butter in a skillet on the grill. 3. Serve open-faced with Golden Onions on burger topped with fried egg. Dust with paprika and serve with ketchup.
Golden Onion	Homemade Burger Buns*	Swiss cheese slices Golden Onions* Sauteed Mushrooms*	ketchup and mustard, if desired	1. After turning burgers, place a slice of cheese on the cooked side. 2. Carry prepared hot onions and mushrooms to picnic in insulated containers. Or prepare in advance, refrigerate up to 2 days and reheat in a small pan on grill while burgers cook. 3. Serve burgers open-faced on bun halves with onions and mushrooms spooned on top.
Grecian Delight	Pita Bread* (page 159)	shredded lettuce or spinach leaves diced tomatoes chopped cucumber crumbled Feta Greek olives	Vinaigrette Dressing (page 190)	1. Heat bread on grill if desired. 2. Line bread pocket with lettuce or spinach, then slip burger in and fill with tomatoes, cucumber, cheese and olives. 3. Sprinkle filling with Vinaigrette Dressing.
Reuben Burgers	Homemade Burger Buns*	sauerkraut	dairy sour cream mixed with a little dill weed and minced onion, or bottled Russian dressing	1. Heat sauerkraut in a small pan on grill or carry to picnic already heated in a small thermal container. 2. Spread sour cream or dressing on the inside of both halves of bun. 3. Place burger on bun half, spoon hot sauerkraut on top of burger and top with remaining bun half.

Burger	Bread	Toppings	Sauces	Preparation Notes
Rajah Burgers	Homemade Burger Buns*	chutney (purchased)	plain yogurt	**1.** Season meat with ½ teaspoon powdered ginger and ½ teaspoon curry powder per pound before forming patties. **2.** Heat chutney in a small saucepan on grill while burgers cook. **3.** Spread yogurt liberally on both halves of bun. **4.** Place cooked burger on bun half and top with spoonful of hot chutney and remaining bun half.
Taco Burger	Pita Bread* (page 159) or large flour tortilla	refried beans or bean dip shredded lettuce chopped tomatoes grated sharp Cheddar cheese	Taco Sauce*	**1.** Heat beans or dip in a small pan on grill as directed on the label. Heat tortilla on grill. **2.** If using Pita Bread, line with lettuce. **3.** Tuck burger into lettuce-lined pita or place on center of tortilla and add lettuce. Spoon in remaining ingredients as desired. **4.** Roll up tortilla, tucking in ends.
Sprouted Burgers	Pita Bread* (page 159)	lettuce leaves Alfalfa Sprouts* (page 195) sunflower seeds	Yogurt-Sour Cream Dressing* (page 191) or Hummus* (page 158)	**1.** Line bread pocket with lettuce leaves. **2.** Tuck grilled patty into pocket. **3.** Spoon in yogurt dressing or Hummus, then sprouts, and sprinkle in sunflower seeds.
Luau Island Burger	English muffin	banana, sliced diagonally green pepper ring	Spicy Barbecue* Sauce mixed with ½ cup drained crushed pineapple	**1.** Brush patties with barbecue sauce while grilling. **2.** Grill muffins in butter. **3.** After turning patty, top cooked side with banana slices and brush with barbecue sauce. Complete cooking. **4.** Serve open-faced with green pepper ring as garnish.

Burger	Bread	Toppings	Sauces	Preparation Notes
Onion Burger	Homemade Burger Buns*	sliced scallions (including part of the green tops) sliced raw mushrooms crisply fried bacon, crumbled	dairy sour cream	**1.** Spoon sour cream over grilled burger. **2.** Sprinkle liberally with sliced scallions and mushrooms, and crumbled bacon.
Mediterranean Vegetable Burger	Whole Wheat Pita Bread* (page 159)	shredded lettuce Swiss cheese slices hot or cold Ratatouille*		**1.** Line bread with lettuce. **2.** Tuck grilled burger into bread with a slice of cheese. **3.** Top with a large spoonful of Ratatouille.

THE BASIC STUFFED BURGER

1 egg
¼ cup milk
1 slice white bread
¼ cup finely chopped onion
2 tablespoons snipped fresh parsley

1 teaspoon salt
¼ teaspoon pepper
1 tablespoon bottled steak sauce
2 pounds ground chuck

1. Beat egg and milk together in a medium-size bowl and crumble bread into mixture. Allow to soak 5 to 10 minutes.

2. Add remaining ingredients and mix together thoroughly. Shape into 12 patties of equal size, about 4 inches in diameter.

3. Place a portion of the selected stuffing (below) on top of each of 6 patties.

4. Place remaining patties on top of stuffing. Barely moisten fingers with water and crimp edges of patties together to encase filling and prevent leaking during cooking.

5. Carefully arrange stuffed patties in a grill basket (see page 26) to prevent breakage. Grill over medium coals 6 to 8 minutes on each side.

6. Serve on buns or rolls with your favorite condiments.

Serves 6

EGGPLANT-RICE STUFFING FOR HAMBURGERS

4 tablespoons olive oil	1½ cups cold water
1 medium-size onion, chopped	¼ cup pine nuts
1 clove garlic, minced	one 4¾-ounce can eggplant
1 tablespoon parsley flakes	appetizer, finely chopped
½ cup raw rice	Parmesan cheese

1. In a heavy skillet, heat oil over low heat and sauté onion, garlic and parsley for 3 to 4 minutes. Add rice and sauté until it is pale gold.

2. Add water to rice mixture and bring to a boil. Reduce heat and simmer, covered, for 20 minutes. Stir in nuts and eggplant. Cook, covered, an additional 5 minutes.

3. Spoon mixture onto the center of a hamburger patty, sprinkle with cheese and cover with second patty. Continue as directed in the recipe for The Basic Stuffed Burger.

Yield: about 2¼ cups

APPLE AND BACON HAMBURGER STUFFING

⅓ cup butter or margarine	1 teaspoon cinnamon
5 to 6 medium-size apples, peeled, cored and diced	½ teaspoon ground cloves
1 cup brown sugar, packed	8 slices bacon, crisply fried and crumbled

1. Melt butter in heavy skillet. Add apples and sprinkle with the sugar and spices. Simmer 6 to 8 minutes, until apples are tender but still hold their shape.

2. Spoon apple mixture onto the center of a hamburger patty, sprinkle with crumbled bacon and cover with second patty. Continue as directed in the recipe for The Basic Stuffed Burger.

Yield: 2½ to 3 cups

HOMEMADE BURGER BUNS

2 packages active dry yeast	1½ teaspoons salt
1 cup warm water (110° to 115°F)	7 to 8 cups sifted all-purpose flour
1 cup warm milk (110° to 115°F)	2 eggs, slightly beaten
6 tablespoons sugar	¼ cup butter or margarine, melted and cooled

1. In a large mixing bowl, dissolve yeast in warm water.

2. In a small bowl, combine warm milk with sugar and salt to dissolve. Mix well, then add to the yeast.

3. Add 2 cups of the flour to the mixture and beat 2 minutes at medium speed with electric mixer. Add ¾ cup flour. Beat at high speed 2 minutes, scraping bowl occasionally. Stir in beaten eggs and melted butter.

4. Stir in enough additional flour to make a stiff dough. Turn out onto a lightly floured board and knead until smooth and elastic, about 8 to 10 minutes.

5. Place dough in a greased bowl, turning to grease the top. Cover and let rise in a warm place until doubled, about 45 minutes. Punch down, cover and let rise again until less than doubled, about 20 minutes.

6. Divide dough into 20 to 24 equal portions and form each portion into a smooth round ball. Place on greased baking sheets about 2 inches apart. Press to flatten. Cover and let rise in a warm place until doubled, about 1 hour.

7. Preheat oven to 375°F. Bake 15 to 20 minutes or until done.

Yield: 20 to 24 buns

GOLDEN ONIONS

3 tablespoons butter or margarine	4 medium-size onions, sliced and separated into rings

1. Melt butter in a large heavy skillet. Add onion rings and cook over medium heat for 30 minutes. Stir occasionally. As onions begin to turn golden, stir more frequently. *Do not allow onions to brown during the first 15 minutes of cooking.*

2. Remove onions from the heat when they are a light, golden color. Serve hot over hamburgers.

Yield: about 1¾ to 2 cups

SAUTEED MUSHROOMS

4   tablespoons butter or
      margarine
½   pound fresh mushrooms,
      sliced
1   teaspoon dried basil
salt and pepper to taste
2   teaspoons lemon juice

1. Melt butter in a heavy skillet. Add remaining ingredients and sauté until mushrooms are cooked through and golden.

2. Serve hot over hamburgers or steak.

Yield: about 1 cup

SPICY BARBECUE SAUCE

⅓   cup vegetable oil
1   medium-size onion, chopped
½   cup light corn syrup
½   cup ketchup
½   cup water
½   cup red wine vinegar
2   tablespoons Dijon-style
      mustard
2   tablespoons
      Worcestershire sauce
2   teaspoons salt
generous grating of fresh
      black pepper

1. Heat oil in a small skillet and sauté onion. Add remaining ingredients and simmer for 15 minutes, stirring occasionally.

2. Brush over burgers or chops while grilling.

Yield: 2 cups

TACO SAUCE

2   medium-size tomatoes,
      peeled, seeded and
      finely chopped
one   4-ounce can green
      chilies, chopped
2   scallions finely chopped
      (including part of the
      green tops)
1   clove garlic, minced
1   teaspoon ground
      coriander
½   teaspoon salt
1   tablespoon olive oil
1   tablespoon lemon juice
dash of hot pepper sauce (or
      more, to your liking)

1. Combine all ingredients and mix well. Cover tightly and place in refrigerator.

2. Spoon over hamburgers or tacos.

Yield: 1 cup

Variation: Just before serving, gently stir in 1 avocado, peeled, pitted and finely diced.

RATATOUILLE

The vegetables for this savory Mediterranean dish are most readily available and at their flavorful best in the summer months but, if carefully prepared without overcooking, Ratatouille can be made and frozen up to 6 months for fall and winter picnics.

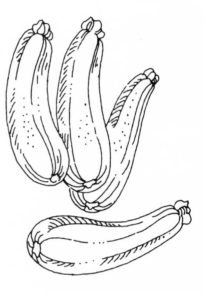

one	½-pound eggplant, peeled and cut into 1-inch cubes	2	cloves garlic, minced
½	pound zucchini, sliced ¼ inch thick	1	pound tomatoes, cut into strips (first cut wedges, then thin strips)
1	teaspoon salt		salt and pepper to taste
4 to 6	tablespoons olive oil	¼	cup chopped fresh parsley
1	large yellow onion, thinly sliced	½	teaspoon dried oregano
		½	teaspoon dried thyme
2	green peppers, seeded and cut into strips	1	teaspoon dried basil

1. Place eggplant and zucchini in separate bowls and add ½ teaspoon salt to each. Toss gently. Let stand for 30 minutes. Drain.

2. Heat oil over medium-high heat in a large, heavy skillet. Sauté eggplant, then zucchini until lightly browned and remove to a large saucepan.

3. In the same skillet, sauté onion, green peppers and garlic until the onion is soft and transparent, about 5 to 10 minutes. Add tomatoes, season with salt and pepper to taste, cover and cook over low heat 5 minutes. Fold in parsley, oregano, thyme and basil.

4. Add tomato mixture to eggplant and zucchini and toss gently to combine. Cover and simmer gently over low heat for 10 minutes. Taste and adjust seasonings if necessary.

5. Raise heat slightly and cook about 15 minutes, until all juices have been absorbed. Do not overcook. If juices do not evaporate completely, lift cooked Ratatouille from the pan with a slotted spoon.

6. Spoon warm or room temperature Ratatouille onto hamburgers. Or it can be served warm as a side dish or chilled as a salad on a bed of lettuce. Ratatouille also makes an excellent stuffing for Tomato Shells (page 92) or a filling for a quiche-like main course (see Ratatouille Pie, page 203).

Yield: about 6 cups

PICNIC BAKED BEANS

two   16-ounce cans pork and beans in tomato sauce
1   cup brown sugar, packed
½   cup ketchup
2   tablespoons prepared mustard
1   medium-size onion, chopped
1   clove garlic, minced
1½   teaspoons ground ginger
6   slices bacon, cut into small pieces and fried

1. Place beans in an ovenproof casserole or in the crock of a slow-cooker. Add remaining ingredients and mix well.

2. Arrange additional slices of bacon on top if desired.

3. Cover and cook in one of the following ways:

a. Bake at 350°F for 1 to 1½ hours. Wrap casserole in several layers of newspaper or transfer to a wide-mouthed thermal container to carry to picnic.

b. Cook over slow campfire coals for 1 to 1½ hours.

c. Cook in the slow-cooker at the low setting for 10 to 12 hours, stirring occasionally. If you put these on to cook at 10:00 P.M., they'll be ready to pack up at 10:00 the next morning for a hearty noontime picnic. Either transfer beans to a thermal container or leave in the slow-cooker crock with the lid secured.

Serves 6 to 8

PEANUT BUTTER COOKIE BARS

⅓   cup creamy peanut butter
one   8-ounce package cream cheese
1   cup brown sugar, firmly packed
1   egg
½   teaspoon baking soda
¼   teaspoon salt
½   teaspoon vanilla
1   cup all-purpose flour
1   cup quick-cooking rolled oats
½   cup chopped unsalted peanuts
1   recipe Chocolate Frosting (page 127)
1   recipe Peanut Butter Glaze (page 127)

1. Preheat oven to 350°F.

2. In a large bowl, beat peanut butter and cream cheese together until fluffy. Add sugar and egg, and mix well.

3. Stir in baking soda, salt and vanilla. Then add flour, rolled oats and peanuts, and blend with electric mixer until mixture holds together in coarse crumbs.

4. Press mixture into a greased 13 × 9 × 2-inch baking pan and bake for 20 to 25 minutes. Cool.

5. Frost with Chocolate Frosting, then drizzle with Peanut Butter Glaze. Cut into bars.

Yield: 12 large bars

CHOCOLATE FROSTING

½ cup butter or margarine	1 pound confectioners'
1 teaspoon vanilla	sugar
⅛ teaspoon salt	½ cup cocoa
	5 to 7 tablespoons milk

1. Cream butter, vanilla and salt together.

2. Gradually add sugar, then cocoa, and mix well. Add enough milk to make a smooth, easily spread frosting.

Yield: about 1½ cups

PEANUT BUTTER GLAZE

¼ cup creamy peanut butter	2 to 4 tablespoons milk
½ cup confectioners' sugar	

1. Beat peanut butter and sugar together until creamy.

2. Add enough milk to make a smooth glaze that will "drizzle" when poured.

Yield: about ½ cup

Autumn Bounty

Best of the Harvest

Labor Day Downeast Clambake

MENU

Steamed Clams

Steamed Lobster

Melted Sweet Butter

Roasted Sweet and Irish Potatoes

Roasted Onions

Ear-Roasted Corn

Beer

Blueberry Yogurt Cake*

Cold Watermelon

Hot Coffee

Beachcombing is the afternoon's activity when a clambake is on the agenda for sundown dining at the shore on Labor Day. You'll need bushels of seaweed and plenty of wood to build a hot, roaring fire to steam live clams and lobsters along with potatoes, onions and fresh corn on the cob. The clambake, an old New England tradition handed down from the Indians, takes all afternoon, so plan it for a leisurely day of camaraderie at the beach with lots of friends. Dinner is ready when the lobsters are bright scarlet and the clams have popped open to reveal their tasty contents. Be sure to save room for dessert—icy chunks of watermelon kept cold in a tub of ice and thick pieces of Blueberry Yogurt Cake accompanied by good hot coffee. I can't think of a better way to end the summer!

DOWNEAST CLAMBAKE

Food Preparation
1   dozen clams per guest
1   lobster per guest
potatoes (sweet and Irish)
onions
corn on the cob
lots of sweet butter

1. The day before the clambake, wash the clams several times and leave in salt water at least 12 hours prior to cooking.

2. Divide the clams into groups of 8 to 12 and wrap them in large squares of cheesecloth.

3. Wrap potatoes and onions in individual cheesecloth squares.

4. To husk the corn, remove the tough outer husk, then gently pull back the inner husks and remove the silk. Re-cover the ear of corn with the husk.

Building and Tending the Cooking Fire

1. Check with local officials about building an open fire on the beach. It might be necessary to obtain a permit.

2. Take along the following supplies and equipment: shovel, bucket, bushel baskets, tarpaulin, rake, asbestos gloves, tongs, nutcrackers.

3. About 3 to 4 hours before you plan to eat, dig a pit in the sand about 1 foot deep and 3 feet across. (The size will depend on the amount of food to be steamed.) Place a layer of flat stones or bricks that have never been used in a fire before in the bottom of the pit.

4. Build a fire using salvaged driftwood and beach refuse in the pit on top of the stones. Keep the fire going for 2 or 3 hours, adding more wood as necessary.

5. Meanwhile, gather several bushels of wet seaweed and soak it in salt water for an hour. You will also need a bucket of salt water handy at cooking time.

6. When the rocks in the bottom of the pit are red-hot and the fire has burned down, it's time to add the seaweed. Rake away the remains of the fire and heap water-soaked seaweed on top of the hot rocks, about 6 inches deep. Add the food in layers with the clams first, then the potatoes, onions, lobster and corn, in that order. Cover the food with another layer of seaweed and sprinkle with a bucket of salt water. Cover the entire pit with a wet tarpaulin weighted down all around with rocks to hold in the steam. Let the foods steam for about an hour. Put butter in a kettle and set it on top of the tarp to melt while the foods cook.

7. When the clams have popped open and the lobsters are bright red, dinner is ready. Rake away the seaweed and let picnickers serve themselves using tongs or asbestos gloves to retrieve the food.

8. Provide each picnicker with a nutcracker for the lobster and a cup to hold melted sweet butter for dipping clams and lobster.

BLUEBERRY YOGURT CAKE

2	cups fresh or frozen blueberries	½	cup butter or margarine, softened
2	cups all-purpose flour	1½	cups dark brown sugar, packed
1	teaspoon baking powder		
½	teaspoon baking soda	3	eggs
½	teaspoon salt	1	teaspoon vanilla
¼	teaspoon cinnamon	1	cup plain yogurt
¼	teaspoon nutmeg	½	cup chopped pecans

Topping

1	teaspoon cinnamon	¼	cup chopped pecans
½	cup brown sugar, packed		

1. Preheat oven to 350°F.

2. Toss blueberries with ¼ cup of the flour and set aside.

3. In a small bowl, mix remaining flour, the baking powder and soda, salt, cinnamon and nutmeg. Set aside.

4. In a large mixing bowl, cream butter and sugar together. Add eggs and vanilla and beat until fluffy. Add flour mixture alternately with yogurt. Beat well after each addition.

5. Stir in blueberries and pecans. Spread batter in a greased 13 × 9 × 2-inch pan.

6. To make topping, mix cinnamon with sugar and pecans. Sprinkle over batter in cake pan. Bake for 45 minutes or until a toothpick inserted in the center comes out clean. Cool in pan.

7. To serve, cut into bars and serve at room temperature.

Serves 12

Variation: Substitute 1 cup chopped fresh rhubarb and 1 cup sliced fresh strawberries for the blueberries.

PICNIC NOTE: This is a good, bake-ahead picnic cake since it tastes better made ahead of time and allowed to sit up to a day before serving. Wrap it airtight to allow the flavors to develop.

Harvest Hayride

When the harvest moon is at its fullest, it's time for a picnic under the stars on top of a wagon full of sweet-smelling hay pulled by two sleepy-eyed horses.

Vegetable Rice Rollups are a great way to take along a salad—the crunchy rice mixture is rolled in pieces of salami. Cold fried chicken, hard-cooked eggs rolled in sausage and deep-fat fried, and a loaf of French bread filled with a tasty meat loaf mixture are all easy to pack and easy to serve along with Glazed Fresh Apple Cookies and Yogurt Cake Brownies for dessert. Carry hot coffee in a thermal container and buy cider and cranberry juice in individual-size bottles for ease in carrying. And don't forget the guitar!

MENU

Vegetable Rice Rollups*

Mother's Oven-Fried Chicken*

French Sandwich Loaf*

Scotch Eggs*

Glazed Fresh Apple Cookies*

Yogurt Cake Brownies*

Hot Coffee

Apple Cider

Cranberry Juice

VEGETABLE RICE ROLLUPS

2 cups water	1½ cups finely chopped celery
1 cup raw rice	½ cup chopped pecans or walnuts
1 beef bouillon cube	salt and pepper to taste
1 tablespoon butter	¾ cup dairy sour cream
1 teaspoon salt	¾ cup plain yogurt
½ cup finely chopped radishes	juice of 1 lemon, or 1 tablespoon prepared lemon juice
⅓ cup finely chopped scallions (including part of the green tops)	
⅓ cup finely chopped green pepper	60 to 75 thin slices Genoa salami

1. Bring water to a boil in a medium-size saucepan. Add rice, bouillon, butter and 1 teaspoon salt. Reduce heat, cover and simmer 20 minutes or until all the water is absorbed by the rice. Allow to cool.

2. Combine vegetables, pecans, seasonings, sour cream, yogurt, lemon juice and cooled rice in a large bowl. Mix well.

3. Place a teaspoonful of the rice mixture in the center of each piece of salami, then fold salami over rice and secure with a toothpick. Refrigerate.

4. Serve as hors d'oeuvres.

Yield: 60 to 75 rollups

NOTE: The rice mixture makes a wonderful stuffing for vegetables like green peppers or Tomato Shells (page 92). Or simply serve the rice mixture on a bed of lettuce for a salad.

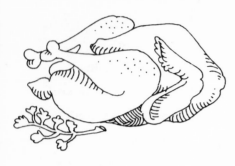

MOTHER'S OVEN-FRIED CHICKEN

½ cup butter or margarine, melted
1 cup all-purpose flour
1 teaspoon salt
⅛ teaspoon pepper
1 teaspoon paprika
one 3-pound frying chicken, cut-up, washed and patted dry

1. Preheat oven to 375°F.

2. Pour melted butter into a 13 × 9 × 2-inch pan.

3. Mix dry ingredients in a small brown paper bag.

4. Shake chicken parts, one or two at a time, in the flour mixture.

5. Place coated chicken pieces, skin side down, in the melted butter.

6. Bake for 30 minutes, then turn pieces skin side up. Bake an additional 30 to 45 minutes, until nicely browned.

7. Serve hot or cold.

Serves 4

FRENCH SANDWICH LOAF

one 8-ounce loaf French bread
1 egg
¼ cup milk
½ cup ketchup
1 pound lean ground beef
1 small onion, chopped
1½ teaspoons prepared mustard
½ teaspoon salt
¼ teaspoon pepper
1 tablespoon parsley flakes
½ teaspoon dried basil
¼ teaspoon oregano
2 tablespoons grated Parmesan cheese

1. Preheat oven to 350°F.

2. Prepare bread by cutting a slit in the underside of the loaf. Carefully remove the bread inside and place in a mixing bowl.

3. Beat egg with milk and ketchup, and pour over bread in bowl. Let stand 5 minutes. Squeeze any excess liquid from the bread.

4. Add remaining ingredients and mix well.

5. Pack bread shell with meat mixture and close opening. Wrap stuffed loaf in foil and bake for about 50 minutes. Or bake 45 minutes and complete at the picnic, placing foil-wrapped loaf in hot coals for 15 to 20 minutes.

6. Serve hot or cold, in slices.

Serves 4 to 6

SCOTCH EGGS

6 hard-cooked eggs, thoroughly cooled and peeled
1 pound ground pork sausage
1 teaspoon Worcestershire sauce
¼ cup dry bread crumbs

¼ cup butter or margarine, melted
1 cup all-purpose flour
2 eggs, beaten
1 cup unseasoned dry bread crumbs
   vegetable oil

1. Place peeled eggs in refrigerator while preparing sausage.

2. Combine sausage with Worcestershire sauce, bread crumbs and as much of the melted butter as necessary to hold the mixture together.

3. Coat each peeled egg with some of the flour, then pat sausage mixture onto each egg.

4. Dip coated egg into remaining flour, then into beaten eggs, and then carefully roll in bread crumbs. Refrigerate for at least 30 minutes if possible.

5. Heat 4 to 5 inches of vegetable oil in a deep saucepan until it reaches 350°F. Fry eggs, one at a time, until golden brown. Drain on paper towels.

Serves 6

GLAZED FRESH APPLE COOKIES

Whenever I make these moist, tender cookies, I automatically double the batch because they disappear so fast. They keep very well when stored in an airtight cookie jar.

½ cup butter or margarine, softened
1⅓ cups brown sugar, firmly packed
½ teaspoon salt
1 teaspoon cinnamon
1 teaspoon ground cloves
1 teaspoon baking soda
1 egg

2 cups sifted all-purpose flour
1 cup chopped walnuts
1 cup chopped red apple (with skin)
1 cup raisins
¼ cup milk
1 recipe Vanilla Glaze (page 134)

1. Preheat oven to 400°F.

2. Cream butter and sugar together until fluffy. Beat in salt, cinnamon, cloves, baking soda and egg.

3. Add 1 cup of the sifted flour and blend well. Then stir in

walnuts, apple, raisins and milk, and mix well. Stir in remaining flour.

4. Drop by rounded teaspoonfuls onto greased baking sheet. Cookies should be spaced 2 inches apart. Bake 11 to 14 minutes, until cookies are evenly browned. Remove to waxed paper.

5. While cookies are still hot, spread thinly with Vanilla Glaze.

Yield: 3 to 4 dozen

Vanilla Glaze

1 tablespoon butter, softened	¼ teaspoon vanilla
	⅛ teaspoon salt
1½ cups confectioners' sugar	2½ tablespoons milk

1. Mix all ingredients together in a small bowl until smooth.

2. Spread carefully on warm cookies.

Yeld: about ¾ cup

YOGURT CAKE BROWNIES

1 cup butter or margarine	¾ cup plain yogurt
1 cup sugar	4 eggs
1 cup dark brown sugar, firmly packed	1 tablespoon vanilla
	1 teaspoon baking powder
three 1-ounce squares unsweetened chocolate, melted	1½ cups all-purpose flour
	1 cup chopped walnuts
	1 cup raisins (optional)

1. Preheat oven to 350°F.

2. Cream butter and sugars together until fluffy. Add melted chocolate and yogurt and mix well.

3. Add eggs one at a time, and beat for 1 minute after each addition.

4. Add vanilla and baking powder and mix well. Stir in flour, then walnuts and raisins (if desired).

5. Spread in a greased 13 × 9 × 2-inch baking pan. Bake for 45 to 50 minutes, or until toothpick inserted in the center comes clean. Cool.

6. Frost, if you wish, with Chocolate Cream Frosting (page 193).

Serves 12

Halloween Afternoon Outing

When the frost is on the pumpkin and the trees have turned to brilliant shades of red and gold, spread your picnic cloth in a sunny spot and dish up mugs of Creamy Pumpkin Soup, served hot from a thermos and sprinkled with mozzarella cheese. The children can cut a sassy jack-o-lantern from the pumpkin shell that carries a crunchy shrimp and vegetable salad to your picnic.

For the sandwich course, choose Groutburgers or Coulibiac, a biscuit-wrapped salmon sandwich loaf, followed by doughnuts and a spicy hot cider drink. Before you head home, enjoy baked apples stuffed with a sweet banana and cranberry mixture or Indian Pudding.

MENU

Creamy Pumpkin Soup*

Groutburgers*
or Salmon Coulibiac* (page 207)

Picnic Pumpkin Treasure Ship*

Sour Milk Doughnuts*

Hot Cider Punch*

Indian Pudding*
or Baked Stuffed Apples*

CREAMY PUMPKIN SOUP

2 cups chopped fresh pumpkin flesh
1 small onion, coarsely chopped
½ cup chopped carrot
2 stalks celery, finely sliced
¼ cup chopped fresh parsley
2 tablespoons butter
three 10¾-ounce cans chicken broth
pinch of dried rosemary
pinch of dried marjoram
pinch of salt
2 egg yolks
½ cup heavy cream
2 teaspoons cinnamon

1. In a heavy 5-quart saucepan, sauté the chopped vegetables and parsley in butter for about 5 minutes.

2. Add chicken broth, rosemary, marjoram and salt. Bring to a boil, then reduce heat, cover and simmer for 1 hour.

3. Purée soup in a blender or beat with an electric mixer at high speed. Fill blender jar only half full and be sure that the lid is tight. The consistency should be creamy. If too thick and grainy, thin with more chicken broth before adding egg and cream mixture.

4. Return purée to the saucepan over low heat.

5. In a small bowl, beat the egg yolks, cream and cinnamon together. Then beat in a little of the hot purée. Pour the beaten mixture into the purée and mix thoroughly.

6. Heat purée, but do not boil. Stir to avoid scorching.

7. If you wish, serve soup hot sprinkled with grated cheese, or serve cold with a dollop of whipped cream and a dash of nutmeg or cinnamon.

Yield: 6 to 8 cups

GROUTBURGERS

These sweet dough buns wrapped around a tasty hamburger and cabbage filling can be made ahead of time and frozen, then reheated or eaten at room temperature.

Sweet Dough Buns

½ cup butter or margarine	½ teaspoon salt
1 cup milk	2 eggs, beaten
2 packages active dry yeast	4 to 4¾ cups sifted all-
½ cup sugar	purpose flour

1. Melt butter in a small saucepan over medium heat. Add milk and heat to 110°F to 115°F.

2. Transfer butter-milk mixture to a large bowl and add yeast. Stir until yeast is completely dissolved. Stir in sugar and salt, then beaten eggs. Add 2 cups of the flour and beat until the dough is smooth and elastic.

3. Add enough of the remaining flour to make a soft but not sticky dough, using hands to complete the mixing if necessary. Turn out onto a lightly floured surface and knead until smooth, soft and elastic.

4. Place dough in a lightly greased bowl, turning to grease top. Cover and let rise in a warm place until doubled, about 1 hour.

5. Preheat oven to 425°F.

6. Divide dough in half and roll out each section into a large rectangle ⅛ to ¼ inch thick. Cut each rectangle into eight squares.

7. Fill the center of each square with Beef and Cabbage Filling (below). Bring the four corners together in the center and seal.

8. Place each completed "bun," sealed side down, on a greased baking sheet and bake 15 minutes, or until evenly browned. Remove to a wire rack to cool.

9. Serve warm or at room temperature.

Yield: 16 filled buns

Beef and Cabbage Filling

2 pounds lean ground beef	2 cups grated raw cabbage
1 small onion, chopped	salt and pepper to taste
6 tablespoons butter or margarine	⅛ teaspoon garlic powder
	2 tablespoons sugar

1. Brown ground beef in a heavy skillet. Drain fat.

2. Sauté onion in 2 tablespoons of the butter. Add to browned meat.

3. Fry cabbage in the remaining 4 tablespoons butter until tender. Add to browned meat. Season meat and cabbage with salt and pepper to taste, garlic powder and sugar. Mix well.

4. Use a slotted spoon to place prepared filling in the dough squares and bake as instructed above.

PICNIC PUMPKIN TREASURE SHIP

one   10-ounce package frozen snow peas, thawed
18   small fresh shrimp (about ⅔ pound— frozen shrimp can be substituted if necessary)
2   scallions (including part of the green tops)
8   radishes, thinly sliced
2   large stalks celery, thinly sliced
2   carrots, thinly sliced
1   medium-size zucchini, thinly sliced

½   cup peanut oil
4   tablespoons cider vinegar
6   tablespoons Japanese soy sauce
1 to 2   teaspoons grated fresh ginger, or ½ teaspoon ground ginger
¼   teaspoon salt
1   tablespoon sugar
one   5- to 6-pound pumpkin
1   tablespoon toasted sesame seeds
½   cup coarsely chopped walnuts
1   cup bean sprouts (page 195)

1. Place thawed snow peas on paper towels to dry.

2. Drop shrimp into 2 cups of boiling salted water and boil 3 to 4 minutes, until pink and firm. Drain in a colander and run cold water over them to stop any additional cooking.

3. Peel shrimp. Make a shallow incision along their backs with the tip of a small, sharp knife. Remove the intestinal vein with the tip of the knife. Cut each shrimp in half crosswise and place in a large bowl.

4. Add the snow peas, scallions, radishes, celery, carrots and zucchini.

5. Combine oil, vinegar, soy sauce, ginger, salt and sugar in a shaker jar and shake vigorously to mix well.

6. Toss shrimp-vegetable mixture with soy sauce dressing, cover and refrigerate for at least 1 hour.

7. Shortly before serving time, cut a scalloped lid from the top of the pumpkin about 4 to 5 inches in diameter. Discard the membrane but save the seeds for a tasty, healthy snack.* If the cavity in

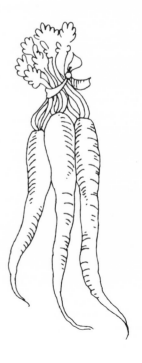

the pumpkin is not large enough to hold the salad mixture, cut some of the flesh from the inside of the pumpkin with a scoop, knife or melon baller. Reserve meat for pie or soup.

8. Spoon marinated salad into the pumpkin and sprinkle with toasted sesame seeds and walnuts. Replace lid.

9. Serve on a bed of crunchy bean sprouts.

Serves 6

PICNIC CRAFT: Be sure to take along a sharp knife and a few paper towels. After the "treasure" has been served from the pumpkin, wipe the interior with the paper towels. Then design and cut your Halloween jack-o-lantern to take home for the front porch or window.

SOUR MILK DOUGHNUTS

3	cups all-purpose flour	½ cup sour milk
¾	cup sugar	2 eggs, well beaten
½	teaspoon nutmeg	1 tablespoon butter or
½	teaspoon salt	margarine, melted
½	teaspoon baking soda	vegetable oil

1. Sift flour, sugar, nutmeg and salt together into mixing bowl.

2. Dissolve baking soda in sour milk. Combine with beaten eggs and stir into flour mixture. Add melted butter and mix well. Chill 15 minutes.

3. On a lightly floured surface, roll out dough to about ½-inch thickness. Cut into rounds with well-floured doughnut cutter. Place doughnuts on absorbent paper and allow to sit 10 minutes.

4. Heat oil to 375°F in a large kettle. Slide doughnuts into kettle, one at a time. Do not crowd kettle with too many doughnuts. Turn doughnuts as soon as they are brown on one side, about 1½ minutes. When evenly brown, remove to absorbent paper with tongs.

5. Allow to cool, then dust with powdered sugar, glaze with your favorite frosting or enjoy them plain.

Yield: 2 dozen

---

*Place pumpkin seeds on a baking sheet in a warm oven and bake until they are dried out, about 1½ to 2 hours. Eat as a snack like sunflower seeds.

HOT CIDER PUNCH

1	quart apple cider or apple juice	1	teaspoon whole allspice
1	quart cranberry cocktail	1½	sticks cinnamon
½	cup brown sugar, packed	6	whole cloves

1. Mix all ingredients together in a large saucepan and bring to a boil. Reduce heat and simmer, covered, for 30 minutes.

2. Strain to remove spices and serve hot.

Yield: about 2 quarts

Variations: Pour Hot Cider Punch over half a glass of a white wine like Pinot Chardonnay or over a rosé. Or add a jigger of vodka or rum to each glass of punch. For a summertime cooler, mix refrigerated punch with an iced lemon-lime soda.

INDIAN PUDDING

4	cups half and half	1	teaspoon cinnamon
5	tablespoons cornmeal	½	teaspoon ground ginger
2	eggs	¼	teaspoon nutmeg
1	cup dark molasses	2	tablespoons butter
1	teaspoon salt	¾	cup cold milk

1. Combine 1 cup of the half and half with the cornmeal in a small bowl. Set aside.

2. In a heavy saucepan, heat the remaining 3 cups of half and half. Add moistened cornmeal and cook, stirring constantly, until mixture begins to simmer. Reduce heat to low and cook for 20 minutes, stirring constantly. Remove from heat.

3. Preheat oven to 325°F.

4. Beat eggs until frothy, then stir in molasses, salt, cinnamon, ginger and nutmeg.

5. Add egg mixture to cornmeal mixture, whip quickly to combine and pour into a buttered 2-quart pudding mold. Pour cold milk over the top. Bake for 1 hour or until a silver knife inserted in the center comes out clean.

6. Cool and unmold, or serve warm from the baking dish with Irene's Vanilla Ice Cream (page 82) made at the picnic.

Serves 6 to 8

BAKED STUFFED APPLES

6 medium-size apples, washed and cored
1 cup finely chopped banana
½ cup whole cranberry sauce
¾ cup brown sugar, packed

1 teaspoon cinnamon
1 tablespoon grated orange rind
butter
brown sugar
boiling water
3 tablespoons orange juice

1. Preheat oven to 375°F.

2. Place cored apples in a buttered glass baking dish.

3. Combine banana, cranberry sauce, sugar, cinnamon and orange rind. Firmly stuff centers of apples with mixture. Top each with a pat of butter and sprinkle with a little brown sugar.

4. Pour boiling water into the bottom of the baking dish and bake for 20 minutes. Baste apples with cooking juice, sprinkle with orange juice and bake an additional 15 minutes or until apples are tender but not mushy. Replenish disappearing liquid with additional orange juice if necessary.

5. Serve hot or cold.

PICNIC NOTE: Carry apples to the picnic in the baking dish if possible, or carefully transfer apples and cooking juices to a hard-sided container just large enough to hold apples close together.

Haute Picnique à la Foliage

What better reason to really splurge on a gourmet picnic than to highlight a leisurely drive through the countryside to enjoy the brilliantly colored fall foliage! Crisp autumn air and the scenic delights of country back roads will surely whet your appetites, so lay out your blanket under a spreading maple and indulge in this splendid repast. Preparation is time-consuming but certainly worth the effort!

WINE-MARINATED MUSHROOMS

Tasty morsels floating in a colorful liquid bath, these are really delicious and you can't beat them for simplicity.

1	pound fresh button mushrooms or large ones, quartered	⅔	cup olive oil
		⅓	cup Burgundy wine
		1	teaspoon garlic salt

1. Thoroughly clean mushrooms with a damp cloth. Trim stems as necessary and place mushrooms in a small bowl.

2. Combine remaining ingredients in a shaker jar and shake vigorously to mix well. Pour over mushrooms. Cover, refrigerate and allow to marinate overnight.

3. To serve, lift from marinade with a slotted spoon.

Yield: about 2 cups

BRUSSELS SPROUTS WITH CREAMY TOMATO DIP

two	10-ounce packages frozen baby brussels sprouts	½	teaspoon salt
		⅛	teaspoon pepper
½	cup vegetable oil	1	teaspoon snipped fresh parsley
2	tablespoons grapefruit juice or orange juice	1	teaspoon snipped chives
½	teaspoon dry mustard		Creamy Tomato Dip (page 142)

1. Cook brussels sprouts according to package directions. Drain.

2. Combine oil with grapefruit juice, mustard, salt, pepper, parsley and chives. Pour over drained brussels sprouts. Cover and refrigerate to marinate at least 1 hour. Stir occasionally.

3. Lift brussels sprouts from marinade, arrange on a platter and serve with Creamy Tomato Dip.

Serves 6

CREAMY TOMATO DIP

2 small tomatoes, peeled, seeded and chopped	1 beef bouillon cube
½ teaspoon dried basil	¼ cup water
½ teaspoon sugar	½ cup dairy sour cream
	½ cup plain yogurt

1. Combine tomatoes with basil, sugar, bouillon cube and water in a small saucepan, and cook to a paste over medium heat. Chill through.

2. Add chilled tomato paste to sour cream and yogurt, and blend well. Refrigerate, covered, for at least 1 hour before serving.

Yield: 1½ cups

HAM-WRAPPED FRUIT TIDBITS

1 whole fresh pineapple	2 papayas
1 pound ham or salami, thinly sliced	1 cantaloupe or honeydew melon

1. Cut pineapple in half lengthwise with a sharp knife. Be sure to leave the crown of leaves intact on both halves.

2. Loosen fruit from pineapple with a sawing motion. Remove fruit, discard the hard fibrous core and cut fruit into 1½-inch chunks.

3. Wrap each piece of pineapple in a small rectangle of ham and secure with a toothpick.

4. Peel and seed papaya and melon. Cut fruit into chunks and wrap in ham as for pineapple.

5. Mound wrapped fruit in pineapple halves, cover with transparent wrap and chill.

6. Serve alone, or use Yogurt-Sour Cream Dressing (page 191) for a dipping sauce, then dip in a small bowl of shredded coconut.

Serves 6 to 8

ARTICHOKE-STUFFED WHOLE TROUT
OR CHICKEN BREASTS

The unusual stuffing in this recipe can be used in trout or chicken for a cold entrée.

For trout:

2   whole trout (with head and tail intact), gutted and cleaned (approximately 1½ pounds each)

salt and pepper

Stuffing

1   orange

one   8½-ounce can artichoke hearts, drained and chopped

¾   cup chopped ripe olives

¼   cup finely chopped onion

½   teaspoon capers, chopped

one   4-ounce jar pimientos, drained and finely chopped

½   cup snipped fresh parsley

1   egg, lightly beaten

1   cup ricotta cheese

½   cup shredded Swiss cheese

½   teaspoon dried basil

¼   teaspoon dried tarragon

salt and pepper to taste

Sauce

½   cup lemon juice

3   tablespoons butter, melted

¼   teaspoon dried tarragon

1. Preheat oven to 450°F.

2. Rinse trout and pat dry. Season with salt and pepper.

3. To make stuffing, grate the orange rind into a medium-size bowl. Remove white pith from orange, then slice orange crosswise and section. Add to orange rind. Add remaining stuffing ingredients and mix well.

4. Divide stuffing between the 2 fish and fill the cavities. Close and secure with toothpicks. Place in a lightly greased baking pan.

5. To prepare sauce for trout, mix all ingredients. Pour over fish. Cover with aluminum foil. Bake for 25 to 30 minutes.

6. Lift from baking dish and serve hot or cold.

Serves 2 to 4

For chicken:

3   whole chicken breasts   salt and pepper
        with bone
        (approximately 3
        pounds)

Stuffing
as for trout

Sauce

½   cup white wine or ½ cup   2   tablespoons butter,
        chicken stock   melted

1. Preheat oven to 350°F.

2. Rinse chicken breasts and pat dry. Season with salt and pepper. Remove the bone without removing the skin. Separate the skin from the flesh of the chicken, leaving it attached at the center of each breast.

3. Prepare stuffing following Step 3, page 143.

4. Place a third of the stuffing under the skin of each chicken breast. Tuck skin edges under and secure with toothpicks if necessary. Place chicken breasts in a lightly greased baking pan skin side up.

5. To prepare sauce for chicken, mix wine and melted butter. Pour over chicken breasts. Bake for 35 to 40 minutes, basting every 10 minutes with the juices. Skin should be nicely browned and the meat fork tender.

6. Serve hot, or chill in refrigerator and slice to serve.

Serves 3 to 6

ORANGES BURGUNDY

6   large seedless oranges,   1   cup Burgundy wine
        peeled and thinly sliced   ½   cup chopped walnuts
½   cup brown sugar, packed

1. Place oranges in a shallow dish and sprinkle with sugar, then cover with wine and chill overnight.

2. Sprinkle with walnuts and serve as a salad on a bed of lettuce.

Serves 6

CURRIED SQUASH PIE

1   recipe Single Crust
    Pastry (page 188)
2   small zucchini, cut into ¼-
    inch slices
1   medium-size onion,
    thinly sliced
¼   pound fresh mush-
    rooms, thinly sliced
1   teaspoon curry powder
1   teaspoon dry mustard

½   teaspoon ground ginger
¼   cup toasted wheat germ
½   cup finely shredded
    Swiss cheese
3   eggs
1   cup milk
2   teaspoons prepared mustard
2   teaspoons Worcestershire
    sauce

1. Preheat oven to 425°F.

2. Prepare pastry according to directions on page 188. Roll out pastry to a 12-inch circle on a lightly floured surface. Fit into a 9-inch pie plate. Trim overhang, turn under and flute edges and prick shell all over with a fork. Bake for 8 minutes. Remove and cool slightly.

3. Decrease oven temperature to 375°F.

4. In a small saucepan, steam zucchini, onion and mushrooms for 5 minutes or until squash is just barely tender. Remove from pan.

5. Mix curry powder, dry mustard, ginger, wheat germ and cheese together in a small bowl.

6. Place half of the steamed vegetables in the bottom of the cooled pastry shell. Sprinkle with half of the spice-cheese mixture. Repeat layers.

7. Beat eggs slightly, then beat in milk, prepared mustard and Worcestershire sauce. Pour mixture over vegetables in pastry. Bake for 40 minutes or until center is almost set but not soft. Custard will set as it cools.

8. Let stand at least 15 minutes before serving.

Serves 6

SUGAR CRUNCH GRAPE TART

Crust

1½ cups very fine graham cracker crumbs

¼ cup finely chopped hazelnuts

6 tablespoons brown sugar

¼ cup light cream

½ cup butter, melted

Filling

2½ to 3 pounds green seedless grapes, washed and stemmed

2½ cups dairy sour cream

½ pound dark brown sugar

1. Preheat oven to 300°F.

2. To make crust, combine crumbs with hazelnuts, sugar, cream and melted butter. Pat crumbs into a 10-inch-diameter deep-dish pie plate. Bake for 15 minutes. Cool.

3. Increase oven temperature to broil.

4. To make filling, combine grapes with sour cream. Spoon into prepared crust.

5. Cover grapes and sour cream with some of the brown sugar. Broil to melt the brown sugar.

6. Repeat this sugaring and broiling process until the sugar is all used and the top of the pie is coated with a crisp sugar crust.

7. Serve hot or chilled.

Serves 6

Homecoming Tailgater

Homecoming weekend is a perfect time to join in the festivities of the football season with a pregame tailgater picnic. Pack up your favorite foods, folding chairs, and a card table if your car doesn't have a tailgate. In the stadium parking lot, spread out the lunch on the tailgate or table and enjoy the open air conviviality with everyone else who planned picnics at the stadium to avoid the game-time traffic rush.

Since fall weather can be unpredictable, most of the foods in this menu have been chosen because they can be served hot or cold, even the bean salad! Included is a spicy mixture of dried fruits and vegetables to carry along to the game for snacking with your favorite hot or cold beverages.

TOMATO JUICE COOLER

1 quart tomato juice	dash of Tabasco sauce
½ cup sugar	lemon or lime wedges
½ cup lemon or lime juice	
1 teaspoon Worcestershire sauce	

1. In a small saucepan, combine tomato juice and sugar. Cook over medium heat until sugar is completely dissolved. Add remaining ingredients. Chill.

2. Serve over cracked ice and garnish with a wedge of lemon or lime.

Yield: 4½ cups

BLOODY MARY MIX

6 cups tomato juice	¼ cup lemon juice
3 tablespoons prepared horseradish	salt and pepper to taste
	vodka
1 to 2 teaspoons Tabasco sauce	celery stalks
2 teaspoons Worcestershire sauce	

1. Combine all ingredients in 2-quart container, mix well, chill.

2. For each serving, pour 1½ ounces of vodka over crushed ice in a tall glass. Add 1 cup of Bloody Mary Mix, stir well and garnish with a celery stalk.

Yield: 6½ cups

WHISKEY-BUTTERED BRIE

½ cup butter	dash of cayenne pepper
¼ cup finely chopped walnuts or cashews	one 4-inch wedge fully ripened French Brie cheese, well chilled
3 tablespoons whiskey	
dash of lemon juice	

1. Cream butter and add remaining ingredients except Brie. Mix well.

2. Remove white crust from the top and side of the chilled wedge of Brie. Cover top and three sides with butter mixture. Place in refrigerator.

3. Remove from refrigerator 1 hour prior to serving and let stand at room temperature. Serve on crackers or rounds of toast as an appetizer. This is also good with fresh fruit.

Serves 4 to 6 as appetizer

PICNIC NOTE: For easy transport to your picnic spot, place buttered Brie in a plastic wedge-shaped storage container with airtight lid.

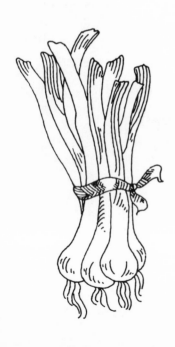

STEAK ROLLUPS

½ cup raw long-grain white rice	2 tablespoons chopped pimiento
¼ teaspoon dried thyme	2 tablespoons butter or margarine
¼ teaspoon dried marjoram	2 pounds round steak
¼ cup sliced scallions (including part of the green tops)	2 tablespoons vegetable oil
	one 10½-ounce can onion soup
¼ cup finely chopped green pepper	1 cup water or dry sherry
6 large fresh mushrooms, finely chopped	

1. Cook rice until tender according to package directions. Stir in thyme, marjoram, scallions, green pepper, mushrooms, pimiento and butter. Mix well and cover.

2. Divide steak into six portions. Pound pieces to approximately 6 × 4 inches.

3. Spread rice filling in the center of each piece of meat. Roll up and fasten with toothpicks.

4. Heat oil in a large heavy skillet. Brown steak rolls in the hot oil. Add soup and water. Cover and simmer 1½ hours.

5. Remove rollups and serve hot, or chill and serve sliced or in French rolls with your favorite condiment.

Serves 6

APPLE-HAM WHEEL

1 recipe Single Crust Pastry (page 188)	6 slices bacon, crisply fried and crumbled
5 cups peeled and sliced tart cooking apples	3 eggs
	1 cup milk
1¼ cups shredded sharp Cheddar cheese	¼ teaspoon ground allspice
	¼ teaspoon ground ginger
1 cup diced boiled ham	½ teaspoon salt

1. Preheat oven to 425°F.

2. Prepare pastry according to directions on page 188. Roll out to a 12-inch circle on a lightly floured surface. Fit into a 9-inch pie pan. Trim overhang, turn under and flute edges and prick shell all over with fork. Bake for 8 minutes. Remove from oven and cool slightly.

3. Decrease oven temperature to 350°F.

4. Arrange half the apple slices in the cooled pastry shell in overlapping circles. Sprinkle with half the cheese, ham and crumbled bacon.

5. Repeat layers with remaining apples, cheese and meats.

6. In a medium-size bowl, beat eggs slightly. Beat in milk, spices and salt. Pour over apple mixture in pie shell. Bake for 50 minutes to 1 hour or until knife inserted in center comes out clean. Do not overbake. Custard will set as it cools.

7. Serve warm or cold as an entrée.

Serves 6

Variation: This dish can also be made with a double crust.

PICNIC NOTE: Carry this main-dish apple pie to the picnic in the pie pan, or cut it into six wedges and wrap each individually in aluminum foil. Pack in a cooler if you won't be eating for several hours.

BASIL BEAN SALAD

The basil in the dressing gives this traditional picnic salad extra tang!

one	15-ounce can chick peas (including canning liquid)	1	clove garlic, minced
		¼	cup red wine vinegar
one	15-ounce can red kidney beans (including canning liquid)	⅓	cup olive oil
		1 to 2	tablespoons brown sugar
one	10-ounce package frozen French-cut green beans, thawed	½	teaspoon salt
		¼	teaspoon pepper
1	cup thinly sliced celery	2	teaspoons dried basil, or 4 tablespoons finely minced fresh basil
1	small red onion, thinly sliced		lettuce leaves
¼	cup finely chopped fresh parsley		tomato wedges

1. In a large bowl, combine beans, celery, onion, parsley and garlic. Mix well.

2. Put remaining ingredients in shaker jar and shake vigorously to mix well.

3. Pour dressing over salad and toss gently. Cover, refrigerate and allow to marinate several hours or overnight.

4. To serve, spread on lettuce leaves in a shallow serving bowl and garnish with tomato wedges.

Serves 6

Variation: This salad is good hot, too, especially for a fall or winter picnic. Place the salad in a saucepan and bring it to a simmer over medium heat, then simmer gently until heated through. Transfer to preheated thermal container.

STEAMED CARROT-RAISIN PUDDING

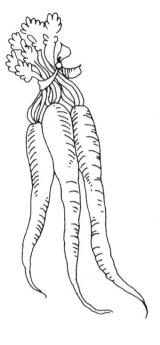

¾ cup brown sugar, packed
⅓ cup butter or margarine
½ cup milk
1 egg
1½ cups sifted all-purpose
flour
2 teaspoons baking powder
½ teaspoon cinnamon
¼ teaspoon ground allspice
¼ teaspoon nutmeg
¼ teaspoon salt
½ cup raisins
½ cup chopped dates
½ cup grated carrot, packed
grated rind and juice of ½
lemon
Apricot Sauce (below)

1. Cream sugar and butter together in mixing bowl.

2. Beat milk and egg together, then add to sugar and butter and mix well.

3. Combine dry ingredients, then add gradually to sugar mixture and mix until well blended. Stir in remaining ingredients except Apricot Sauce. Mix thoroughly.

4. Spoon into greased pudding mold or a 1-pound coffee can, cover and place on a rack in a large pan. Pour in 1 to 2 inches of water. Bring to a boil, then lower heat and steam for 3 hours. Toothpick inserted in center should come clean. Allow to cool slightly, then remove from mold. Refrigerate.

5. Slice and serve with Apricot Sauce.

Serves 6 to 8

APRICOT SAUCE
¼ cup butter
1 cup confectioners' sugar
½ cup canned apricots,
drained
½ teaspoon vanilla

1. Cream butter and sugar together.

2. Purée apricots in blender. Add to sugar and butter mixture and mix well. Stir in vanilla.

Yield: about 1 cup

Variation: Fold fruit mixture into 1 cup heavy cream, which has been whipped, before serving over dessert. Sauce must be refrigerated if cream is added.

SWEET AND SPICY ENERGY CRUNCH

Based on an Indian snack, this is a tasty alternative to the traditional "gorp" carried by campers and backpackers.

¼ cup dried lentils
¼ cup raw long-grain white rice
¼ cup dried split peas
3 cups water
2 tablespoons peanut oil
1 tablespoon sesame seed
1 tablespoon curry powder (mild or hot, to your liking)

½ cup roasted salted peanuts
½ cup roasted salted cashews
½ cup golden raisins
¼ cup roasted sunflower seeds
½ cup shredded coconut
¼ teaspoon ground cloves
pinch of cayenne pepper

1. Rinse lentils, rice and peas, and place in a large saucepan with the water. Bring to a boil and boil for 1 minute. Remove from heat, cover and set aside for 10 minutes. Drain and rinse with cold water, then spread on paper towels and pat dry.

2. Heat oil in a large heavy skillet over medium heat. Add lentils, rice, peas, sesame seed and curry powder, and cook, stirring until toasted, about 10 to 15 minutes. Remove from heat and stir in remaining ingredients. Mix well.

3. Store in an airtight container up to a week.

4. To serve, pour into serving bowl. Scoop up individual servings with chips or crackers or simply use your fingers.

Yield: 2½ cups

Middle East Feast

The foods included in this picnic menu are typical of those that would be served as appetizers or the first course of a Middle Eastern meal. This appetizer course is called *Mezze* (met-see). Served with a main dish like Shish Kebab (page 209), traditional *Mezze* foods make great picnic fare because they are meant to be eaten with the fingers—no utensils, please. In some Middle Eastern countries, it is traditional to use only the thumb and first two fingers of the hand to eat these foods. Anyone who uses additional fingers is considered a glutton! The *Mezze* foods are shared by most of the Middle Eastern countries, including Lebanon, Syria, Greece, Turkey and Tunisia. One or two ingredients and the spelling for each dish might vary slightly, but these foods are substantially the same throughout the region. Buy the unusual ingredients for these dishes at your local deli, in the specialty food section of your supermarket or in a specialty food store.

Middle Eastern food is typically served at a low, round table, but an old card table with the legs cut down and the top covered with a bright cloth will suffice for picnic purposes. Or spread your picnic on a rug of Middle Eastern design. Use brass trays and bowls and woven baskets for serving dishes to add to the atmosphere.

MENU

Chunks of Honeydew Melon

Stuffed Grape Leaves*

Cheese and Spinach Pie*

Tabooli with Romaine Leaves*

Hummus*   Lavash*

Pita Bread*

Greek Olives

Iced Mint Tea

Retsina or Pinot Chardonnay Wine

Greek Cookies*

Baklava (purchased)

Pistachio Nuts

STUFFED GRAPE LEAVES (Yaprak Dolmasi)

1	quart grape leaves	¼	cup currants, washed and drained
4	tablespoons olive oil	1	tablespoon dried mint leaves
1	clove garlic, chopped	1	teaspoon sugar
1	medium-size onion, chopped	1	teaspoon ground allspice
1½	cups raw brown or short-grain white rice	1	teaspoon pepper
2	medium-size tomatoes, chopped	1	teaspoon salt
3	cups boiling water or chicken broth	¼	cup olive oil
¼	cup pine nuts	¼	cup lemon juice
		½	cup water

1. Carefully separate grape leaves, rinse in warm water and place on wire racks to dry while you prepare the pilaf filling.

2. Heat 4 tablespoons oil in a large heavy skillet. Add garlic and onion and sauté until onion is golden brown. Add rice and tomatoes and sauté for 5 minutes.

Greek Cookies, Lavash and Pita Bread can also be purchased at supermarkets or specialty food stores if you don't have time to make all the dishes in this picnic. Retsina is a traditional Greek wine with a somewhat resiny taste. Pinot Chardonnay also complements the spicy foods in this menu.

3. Add boiling water, pine nuts, currants, mint, sugar, allspice, pepper and salt. Simmer, covered, for about 30 minutes or until rice has absorbed the liquid. Remove from heat.

4. Preheat oven to 350°F.

5. Stuff grape leaves with pilaf filling. Place each leaf on the working surface with the thick-veined side up and the stem toward you. Place a heaping teaspoon of pilaf in the center of the leaf near the stem. Loosely fold sides over filling and roll up into cigar-shaped rolls. To roll, start at stem and roll away from you. Keep making rolls until all filling is used.

6. Line baking dish with grape leaves. (Use broken ones if your first attempts at rolling were unsuccessful.)

7. Place rolls in the lined baking dish, seam side down and close together. Pour ¼ cup oil, the lemon juice, and ½ cup water over the rolled leaves and cover. Bake for 45 minutes.

8. Serve warm or at room temperature.

Serves 8 to 10

Variation: The pilaf filling for grape leaves can also be used to fill several other tasty vegetables including cabbage leaves, tomatoes, green peppers and small Italian eggplants. Follow the general directions and the chart below for special preparation techniques for each vegetable.

General Directions
1. Prepare pilaf stuffing as directed for Stuffed Grape Leaves, Steps 2 to 3, above. Omit mint in pilaf intended for stuffing cabbage.

2. Prepare selected vegetables for stuffing as directed in chart (page 155).

3. Place stuffed vegetables close together in a heavy cooking pan fitted with a lid. Sprinkle with salt and 2 tablespoons olive oil.

4. Pour ½ cup boiling water down the inside of the pan. Cover and simmer for the time specified in the chart.

5. Cool in the pan, then refrigerate. Bring to room temperature 1 hour prior to serving.

Vegetable	Preparation	Cooking Variation	Cooking Time
cabbage (3 to 4-pound head)	**1.** Separate leaves from head of cabbage. **2.** Cook leaves in boiling salted water until pliable, about 5 minutes. Drain on rack. **3.** Cut out hard portion of leaf, overlap cut edges and fill and roll as for grape leaves.	**1.** Pour the olive oil into bottom of pan before arranging rolls. **2.** Place a heatproof plate on top of rolls. **3.** Cool before removing plate.	20 minutes
tomatoes (about 10 small, ripe but firm)	**1.** Cut off tops, remove pulp with small spoon and add pulp to filling mixture. **2.** Stuff seven-eighths full and replace top.	**1.** Place a cake rack in bottom of heavy cooking pan. **2.** Arrange tomatoes close together on rack. **3.** Cook until tomatoes are tender.	15 to 20 minutes
peppers (10 small green)	**1.** Cut off a top slice, remove core and seeds. **2.** Stuff seven-eighths full and replace top.	Same as for grape leaves. Cook until peppers are tender.	25 to 30 minutes
eggplants (8 to 10 small, finger-shaped Italian)	**1.** Remove stems, cut in half and hollow out pulp carefully. **2.** Fill hollow seven-eighths full.	**1.** Cover ends with foil. **2.** Add water if needed to prevent sticking. **3.** Cook until eggplants are tender.	15 to 20 minutes

PICNIC NOTE: Pack Stuffed Grape Leaves (or Stuffed Cabbage) in layers in a hard-sided container with lid. Other stuffed vegetables should be packed close together in a single layer in a similar container.

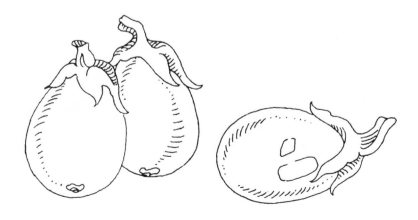

CHEESE AND SPINACH PIE (Spanakopitta)

4 tablespoons olive oil	½ teaspoon salt
1 bunch scallions, chopped (including part of the green tops)	¼ teaspoon pepper
	2 tablespoons dried dill
	½ cup chopped fresh parsley
two 10-ounce packages frozen spinach, thawed, drained dry and finely chopped, or 2 pounds fresh spinach, washed, drained dry and finely chopped	½ pound Feta cheese, finely crumbled
	5 eggs, lightly beaten
	½ pound butter, melted
	16 sheets (½ pound) *filo* pastry or strudel leaves

1. In a large skillet fitted with a lid, heat oil and sauté scallions until tender.

2. Add chopped spinach, cover tightly and cook for 5 minutes. Add salt, pepper, dill and parsley, and cook uncovered 10 minutes, stirring vigorously and constantly. Remove from heat when almost all of the liquid has evaporated. Transfer mixture to a mixing bowl and allow to cool to room temperature.

3. Add cheese and beat in eggs slowly. Adjust seasonings.

4. Preheat oven to 300°F.

5. Brush a 13 × 9 × 2-inch baking pan with a little melted butter.

6. Unfold *filo* pastry and place under a damp (not wet) towel to prevent drying while you work.

7. Carefully remove one sheet of pastry at a time and line the baking pan, being sure to press the edges of the *filo* into the corners and against the sides of the dish. Brush with 2 or 3 teaspoons melted butter.

8. Continue layering filo and brushing with melted butter until the baking dish contains eight layers of buttered pastry.

9. Carefully spread the spinach mixture evenly over the layered *filo*. Then continue *filo* layering process until eight additional layers have been added. Be sure to brush the last layer with butter and trim away any pastry overhang so that it is even with the inside edge of the baking dish.

10. With a sharp knife, mark the top pastry lightly in serving-size squares and cut through the first two or three top layers of pastry. Bake in the middle of the oven for 1 hour, until pastry is brown and puffed.

11. Cool slightly, cut into squares and serve warm, at room temperature or cold.

Serves 12

Variations: This same filling can also be prepared in quiche-fashion, using a pastry shell as described for Ratatouille Pie (page 203). The filling should be enough to fill two prepared shells. Bake at 350°F for 30 to 45 minutes, until set. For a meatier meal, add 1 pound lean ground beef or lamb, browned and drained, to the spinach mixture before adding the cheese and eggs.

PICNIC NOTE: Bake Cheese and Spinach Pie in a baking pan fitted with a slide-on cover for the easiest transport to picnic. Be sure to take along a narrow spatula for serving.

TABOOLI WITH ROMAINE LEAVES

2 cups fine bulghur or cracked wheat
½ cup finely chopped fresh mint, or 2 tablespoons crumbled dried mint leaves
½ cup finely chopped fresh parsley
3 scallions, minced (including part of the green tops)
2 medium-size tomatoes, peeled and finely chopped
1 clove garlic, crushed
½ cup olive oil
juice of 3 lemons (about ⅓ cup)
salt and pepper to taste
crisp romaine leaves
tomato wedges
fresh mint sprigs

1. Soak bulghur in enough water to cover for 30 minutes. Drain well and squeeze out excess moisture. Place in a large salad bowl.

2. Add remaining ingredients except romaine, tomato wedges and mint sprigs. Toss well with two forks. Adjust seasonings. Add more lemon juice if desired. Refrigerate at least 3 hours or overnight to develop flavors.

3. Serve in a large bowl and garnish with tomato wedges and mint. Let picnickers roll up scoops of the salad in romaine leaves or scoop it into Pita Bread (page 159).

Serves 6 to 8

HUMMUS

one 20-ounce can chick peas	½ cup lemon juice
½ cup tahini*	salt to taste
1 clove garlic, crushed	dash of cayenne pepper

1. Drain chick peas and reserve liquid.

2. Place chick peas in blender with tahini and purée, adding enough of the reserved liquid to make a smooth paste.

3. Transfer purée to a small bowl. Add garlic, lemon juice, salt to taste and cayenne.

4. Serve as a dip with Lavash (below) or raw vegetables, or as a spread or sauce for sandwiches and hamburgers.

Yield: about 3 cups

LAVASH (Armenian Cracker Bread)

1 package active dry yeast	½ teaspoon salt
¾ cup warm water (110° to 115°F)	2 cups all-purpose flour

1. Sprinkle yeast over warm water. Stir to dissolve.

2. Add salt and enough flour to make a stiff dough.

3. Knead on a lightly floured surface for about 10 minutes, until dough is smooth and elastic.

4. Place dough in a greased bowl, turning to grease top. Cover and let rise in a warm place until doubled, about 45 minutes. Punch down, cover and let rise again until doubled, about 30 minutes.

5. Preheat oven to 425°F.

6. Divide dough into four balls. Roll out each ball on a floured surface to a 9-inch circle. Place each "loaf" on an ungreased baking sheet and bake one at a time for 7 minutes or until the bread is dry, lightly browned and blistered. Cool. Store in a dry place.

7. Cut into wedges and serve with Hummus (above) or other favorite vegetable dip.

Yield: 4 "loaves"

*Tahini is sesame paste which is available at some supermarkets in the gourmet food section and in most specialty food stores.

PITA BREAD (Pocket Bread)

1 package active dry yeast	1¼ cups warm milk (110° to 115°F)
3 cups all-purpose flour	
¼ teaspoon sugar	1½ tablespoons olive oil
1½ teaspoons salt	

1. In a large bowl, mix yeast with 1½ cups of the flour, the sugar and salt.

2. Add milk and olive oil and beat at the low speed of the electric mixer for 30 seconds. Then beat 3 minutes at high speed. Stir in enough of the remaining flour to make a moderately stiff dough.

3. Knead dough on a floured surface until it is smooth and elastic, about 10 minutes.

4. Place dough in a greased bowl, turning to grease top. Cover and let rise in a warm place until doubled, about 1 hour and 15 minutes. Punch down dough, cover and let rest 10 minutes.

5. Divide dough into eight equal pieces and shape into balls. Roll out each ball on a floured surface to a 6-inch circle. Place dough circles on ungreased baking sheets, cover and let rise in a warm place for 1 hour.

6. Preheat oven to 500°F.

7. Bake on the lowest rack in the oven for about 7 minutes. Bread should be slightly puffed and lightly browned.

8. Serve warm, or cool and store in plastic bags in the refrigerator up to 3 weeks. Pita Bread can also be frozen.

9. To use Pita, slice along the edge of the bread halfway around to open the pocket. Large Pitas can be cut in half crosswise to create two half-round pockets to fill with sandwich fixings or dips.

Yield: 8 Pitas

Variation:

WHOLE WHEAT PITA BREAD

1 package active dry yeast	1¼ cups warm milk (110° to 115°F)
1 cup whole wheat flour	
¼ teaspoon sugar	1½ tablespoons olive oil
1½ teaspoons salt	2 cups all-purpose flour

1. In a large bowl, mix the yeast with whole wheat flour, sugar and salt.

2. Add milk and oil and beat at the low speed of the electric mixer for 30 seconds. Then beat 3 minutes at high speed. Stir in 1¾ cups of the all-purpose flour and mix well.

3. Spread remaining ¼ cup flour on a flat surface and turn dough onto floured surface. Knead until smooth and elastic, about 10 minutes.

4.–9. As described for Pita Bread, page 159.

GREEK COOKIES (Kourabiethes)

1 cup margarine	1 cup chopped almonds
1 cup sweet butter	1 teaspoon baking powder
1 cup confectioners' sugar, sifted	4½ cups sifted all-purpose flour
2 egg yolks, lightly beaten	confectioners' sugar
2 teaspoons vanilla or brandy	

1. Cream margarine and butter together and beat for 10 minutes, until light and creamy and almost white in color.

2. Beat in 1 cup sugar, the beaten egg yolks and vanilla. Stir in almonds and baking powder. Blend in flour. Cover and chill 1 hour.

3. Preheat oven to 425°F.

4. Shape dough into crescents or balls (1½ inches in diameter) and place on an ungreased baking sheet. Bake for 12 to 15 minutes, until cookies are golden brown.

5. Sift confectioners' sugar on a large sheet of waxed paper and carefully remove cookies from baking sheet to sugared sheet. Sift additional confectioners' sugar over the tops and sides of the cookies.

6. Cool thoroughly before storing in an airtight container.

Yield: 4 to 6 dozen, depending on size and shape

PICNIC NOTE: Carry in individual paper baking cups packed in a single layer in a container or in muffin tins. Or carefully layer cookies in a hard-sided covered container just large enough to accommodate them.

Winter Picnics
By Snowbank or Hearth

Winter Office Picnic

The last thing anyone expects for a business luncheon is a picnic! But why not? When you're in the middle of a heavy schedule or hectic day at the office, what could be more refreshing than to break for a hearty homemade lunch spread out in a vacant conference room or on your desk. The relaxing atmosphere that's bound to evolve will certainly help your digestion and send you back to your afternoon commitments in a cheerful frame of mind. The added bonus, of course, is that you won't have to brave the winter cold for a trek to a local restaurant or endure the normal lunchtime tension and noise of a busy establishment.

Add to the picnic atmosphere by spreading the lunch on a bright tablecloth pulled from the pocket of the picnic tote in which you packed the food. This menu revolves around cold foods—artichokes stuffed with a tangy shrimp filling and large wedges of Italian Sausage Pie, a wonderful dense picnic food that can be eaten from the hand. Dessert is simple but special. Splurge on a basket of the biggest, freshest strawberries you can find, then dip them in sour cream and brown sugar—sheer ecstasy!

MENU

Shrimp-Stuffed Artichokes*

Port Cheddar Cheese Spread*
with Rye Bread

Italian Sausage Pie*

Lemon Oatmeal Macaroons*

Brown Sugar Strawberries*

Hot Spiced Coffee* (page 198)

SHRIMP-STUFFED ARTICHOKES

6 medium-size artichokes	2 tablespoons finely chopped fresh parsley
3 tablespoons lemon juice	2 tablespoons finely chopped scallion (including part of the green tops)
1 teaspoon salt	
2½ tablespoons olive oil	
2½ tablespoons lemon juice	
½ teaspoon salt	
¼ teaspoon dried tarragon	one 10¼-ounce can tiny shrimp, drained
1 clove garlic, minced	

1. Cut stems from artichokes and pull off and discard the tough bottom row of leaves. Use kitchen shears to cut ¼ inch from the tops of the leaves.

2. Place 3 tablespoons lemon juice in a large saucepan and dip the cut edges of each artichoke in the juice to avoid discoloration.

3. Set artichokes side by side, stem side down, in the saucepan. Add 1 teaspoon salt and enough boiling water to cover. Simmer,

covered, until the outer leaves pull off easily, about 40 minutes. Do not overcook. Remove artichokes from water, cool slightly and refrigerate several hours to chill.

4. In a medium-size bowl, mix together remaining ingredients except shrimp. Add shrimp and mix well. Cover and chill.

5. Remove artichokes from refrigerator. Gently spread leaves open and *carefully* remove the prickly-pointed inner leaves and the fuzzy choke.

6. Spoon marinated shrimp mixture into the center of each artichoke.

7. Arrange on a platter and serve with Mustard Mayonnaise (page 190), or Yogurt-Sour Cream Dressing (page 191).

Serves 6

Variations: Try the marinated shrimp mixture as an alternate stuffing for Tomato Shells (page 92) or simply as a salad in a leaf of Boston or butter lettuce. Or use it to fill avocado halves, topped with a dollop of the Yogurt-Sour Cream Dressing.

PICNIC NOTE: Wrap each stuffed artichoke carefully in foil and place them in a deep-sided container with an airtight lid. Pack in a picnic cooler. Keep the mayonnaise or yogurt dressing chilled until serving time.

PORT CHEDDAR CHEESE SPREAD

1 pound Port Cheddar cheese, at room temperature	2 cloves garlic, pressed
	4 ounces cashews, finely chopped
two 3-ounce packages cream cheese	

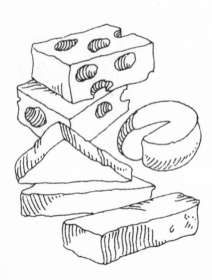

1. Cut Cheddar into chunks and place in mixing bowl with cream cheese. Add garlic.

2. With electric mixer at medium speed, beat cheeses and garlic together to combine.

3. Stir cashews into cheese mixture. Cover and refrigerate.

4. Serve as a cheese spread on rye, pumpernickel or other favorite bread with ham, turkey or chicken.

Yield: about 1½ pounds

Variations: Use this spread as a dip for vegetables. Or shape it into "cheese logs," slice and serve the cheese on round crackers garnished with green olives.

ITALIAN SAUSAGE PIE

1 recipe Double Crust Pastry (page 188)	1 pound mozzarella cheese, shredded
1 pound sweet Italian sausage links, sliced	⅔ cup ricotta cheese
6 eggs	½ teaspoon salt
½ pound fresh mushrooms, sliced	⅛ teaspoon pepper
1 large onion, coarsely chopped	1 clove garlic, minced
one 10-ounce package frozen chopped spinach, thawed	1 tablespoon water

1. Preheat oven to 375°F.

2. Prepare pastry according to directions on page 188. Divide dough into two approximately equal portions, then roll out the large portion to a 12-inch circle. Fit into a 10-inch deep-dish pie plate. Set aside.

3. In a heavy skillet, brown the sausage over medium heat. Drain the fat.

4. Separate 1 of the eggs and set yolk aside. Lightly beat together remaining eggs and the extra egg white. Stir in the browned sausage, the mushrooms, onion, spinach, mozzarella, ricotta, salt, pepper and garlic.

5. Spoon sausage mixture into the pastry-lined pie plate. Roll out the remaining dough to an 11-inch circle. Prick pastry all over and cut slits in it to allow steam to escape during baking. Cover the sausage mixture with pastry, trim overhang and turn under and flute edges of pastry.

6. Combine reserved egg yolk with water and brush on the top crust with a pastry brush. Bake for 1 hour and 15 minutes. Let stand 10 minutes before serving.

7. Serve warm, or refrigerate to chill before serving.

Serves 6 to 8

Variation: Use the same ingredients to make individual tarts.

LEMON OATMEAL MACAROONS

½ cup butter or margarine
one 4-ounce package lemon
   pudding mix
1 cup all-purpose flour
½ teaspoon baking soda
1 teaspoon baking powder
3 tablespoons brown sugar,
   packed

¾ cup quick-cooking rolled
   oats
½ cup shredded coconut
1 egg
1 teaspoon milk
grated rind of ½ lemon

1. Preheat oven to 425°F.

2. In a small pan, melt the butter. Add the pudding mix and cook over medium heat just long enough to dissolve the mix (and the lemon flavoring bead and disk that might come in the mix).

3. Combine remaining dry ingredients in medium-size mixing bowl. Beat in egg and milk, then stir in the pudding mixture and lemon rind.

4. Form dough into small balls and place on an ungreased baking sheet. Press flat with a fork in a crisscross pattern.

5. Bake for 10 to 12 minutes or until delicately browned and just firm. Cool on racks.

Yield: about 4 dozen

BROWN SUGAR STRAWBERRIES

Fresh strawberries in the winter are a pure delight for a special picnic.

1 pint strawberries
1 to 2 cups dairy sour
   cream or plain yogurt,
   or a combination of both

brown sugar

1. Wash strawberries but do not hull. Pile into the berry basket or a small bowl.

2. To serve, dip strawberries in sour cream or yogurt, then in brown sugar.

Serves 2 to 4

Smørrebrød Smörgasbord

Smørrebrød, literally translated from the Danish, means buttered bread. To most people who love food, it means colorful, appetizing, open-faced Danish sandwiches. They are assembled on top of single slices of dense, firm breads like rye, pumpernickel and whole wheat which have first been treated to a coating of sweet butter to prevent sogginess. Depending on the ingredients used, each can be a meal in itself. Because of the nature of this type of sandwich, it makes a perfect do-it-yourself picnic food. Besides buttered bread, smørrebrød sandwiches are made with special spreads, cheeses, meats and seafood, and colorful garnishes like radish slices and lemon wedges. The possible combinations are endless. Good Danish beer and a sweet dessert are all that are needed to round out the menu.

Preparation is minimal. Consider conducting a sandwich-making contest in conjunction with this picnic meal. Ask each picnicker to prepare a sandwich from the ingredients offered to be judged for originality and, most importantly, appetizing appearance. Choose a judge or take a vote and award the winner a six-pack of Danish beer or a large chunk of Danish cheese—Esrom, Danbo or Samsoe for example.

MENU

Wedges of Brie and Jarlsberg Cheese

Rye Crackers

Smørrebrød*

Beet Salad*

Cold Danish Beer

Fresh Fruit

Chocolate Cream Cheese Pie*

Coffee

GENERAL PREPARATION AND PACKING

The chart on page 166 contains several suggestions for spreads, toppings and garnishes that are suitable for the types of bread normally used for smørrebrød. These are only suggestions upon which you are free to build. Recipes for those items starred in the charts are included here or on the pages indicated in parentheses.

1. Use homemade breads at least a day old, or purchase day-old bread at a local bakery. Offer at least two kinds, three if possible.

2. Whip butter and prepare desired spreads and a variety of colorful garnishes. Pack each separately in individual, airtight, colorful plastic containers that can be used for serving.

3. Choose a variety of toppings from the chart and arrange on a colorful serving platter. Cover with transparent wrap. Be sure to trim meats and cheeses to fit bread before arranging on platter.

4. Pack prepared ingredients in a thermal picnic cooler with the platter of toppings in a level position on top.

5. Be sure to pack a bread knife for slicing the loaves and ample utensils for serving and preparing the sandwiches.

SMØRREBRØD SANDWICH CHART

Bread	Spreads	Toppings	Garnishes
Rye	butter and mustard	Tilsit cheese	radish slices
	butter	Crab Salad* asparagus spears	lemon slice sprig of watercress

	butter	thinly sliced smoked
		  salmon
		Marinated Mushrooms*
		  (page 92)
			Mayonnaise* (page 190)
			sprig of fresh dill

	butter
	Avocado Cream Cheese*
	  or Avocado Nut Butter*
	  (page 73)
		tiny shrimp	cherry tomato
			sprig of fresh parsley

	Shallot Butter* (page 195)	smoked salmon Brie cheese	Orange Marinated Onions* sprig of watercress
Pumpernickel	butter	tiny shrimp	twisted lemon slice sprig of fresh dill
	butter sour cream	thinly sliced roast pork	shredded red cabbage sieved egg yolk prune
	butter	pickled herring slices of hard-cooked egg	Orange Marinated Onions* pimiento strips
	butter	liverwurst crisp bacon slices	sliced mushrooms
	Blue Cheese Butter*	spinach leaves shredded chicken breast	crumbled crisply fried bacon

French	butter
	sour cream
		sliced roast beef
		thinly sliced
		  cucumber and onion
			Cucumber-Horseradish Sauce*
			  (page 90)

	butter horseradish Dijon-style mustard	Picnic Potato Salad* (page 79) sardines	sieved egg yolks sprig of fresh parsley
Whole Wheat	butter	egg salad tomato slices	sprig of fresh parsley

Try Sandwich Butter (page 195), French Herb Butter (page 194) or Italian Herb Butter (page 194) as alternatives for plain sweet butter on any of these sandwiches.

AVOCADO CREAM CHEESE

one 3-ounce package cream cheese	1 tablespoon lime juice
1 medium-size ripe avocado, peeled, halved, pitted and mashed	3 tablespoons finely chopped onion
	½ teaspoon salt
	½ teaspoon garlic salt

1. Beat cream cheese and avocado together in a small bowl until smooth. Stir in remaining ingredients.

2. Use as a spread for sandwiches.

Yield: about ⅓ cup

BLUE CHEESE BUTTER

⅓ cup butter or margarine, softened	1 tablespoon Worcestershire sauce
¼ cup crumbled blue cheese	¼ teaspoon garlic salt

1. Beat all ingredients together until creamy and well blended. Refrigerate in a small, airtight container.

2. Use on sandwiches in place of plain butter. Try it on baked or roasted potatoes, too.

Yield: ½ cup

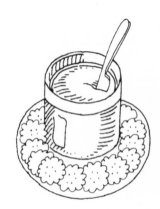

CRAB SALAD

one 7-ounce can shredded crabmeat	¼ cup finely snipped fresh parsley
1 hard-cooked egg, cooled, peeled and finely chopped	juice of 2 lemons
	1 cup Mayonnaise (page 190)
1 small onion, finely chopped	1 tablespoon prepared mustard
1 stalk celery, finely chopped	1 tablespoon ketchup
1 small green pepper, seeded and finely chopped	1 teaspoon chili sauce
	½ teaspoon bottled steak sauce
1 medium-size carrot, finely grated	salt and pepper to taste
	pinch of dried savory

1. Combine crabmeat with egg, vegetables, parsley and lemon juice. Toss to mix well.

2. Combine remaining ingredients, then fold enough of the mixture into the crab and vegetables to moisten well. Add more Mayonnaise if mixture is too dry.

3. Serve as a salad on a leaf of lettuce garnished with a tomato wedge, or use as a sandwich spread.

Serves 4 to 6 as salad or sandwich spread

ORANGE MARINATED ONIONS

3	large red onions, thinly sliced	2	teaspoons grated orange rind
2	tablespoons red wine vinegar	1½	teaspoons salt
1	tablespoon orange juice	1	teaspoon sugar

1. Toss all ingredients together. Cover and chill for several hours.

2. Serve as a side dish, or drain and serve in sandwiches.

Yield: about 1½ cups

BEET SALAD

2	large eating oranges	1	teaspoon brown sugar
one	16-ounce jar sliced beets, drained	½	cup salad oil
1	large red onion, sliced	¼	cup red wine vinegar
2	large stalks celery, sliced	2	teaspoons water
1	tablespoon grated orange rind		lettuce
		2	tablespoons finely chopped pecans

1. Peel oranges, making sure to remove all the white pith. Then slice oranges into circles about ¼ inch thick.

2. Layer oranges, beets, onion and celery in salad bowl.

3. Blend remaining ingredients except lettuce and pecans in shaker jar and shake vigorously to mix well.

4. Pour dressing over layered fruit and vegetables. Cover and refrigerate.

5. Serve on a bed of lettuce. Sprinkle with chopped pecans.

Serves 6

CHOCOLATE CREAM CHEESE PIE

So rich you'll only want a sliver of a piece, this pie easily serves eight to ten picnickers.

1 cup semisweet chocolate pieces	2 eggs, separated
two 3-ounce packages cream cheese, softened	1 teaspoon vanilla
	1 cup heavy cream, whipped
⅛ teaspoon salt	1 recipe Chocolate Crumb Crust (below)
¾ cup brown sugar, packed	

1. Melt chocolate in the top of a double boiler over hot water. Cool 10 minutes.

2. Whip cream cheese and salt until light and fluffy. Gradually add ½ cup of the brown sugar and cream thoroughly. Blend in egg yolks, one at a time, beating well after each addition. Add melted chocolate and vanilla and beat thoroughly.

3. Beat egg whites to soft peaks in a large clean bowl. Gradually add the remaining ¼ cup brown sugar. Beat until egg whites are glossy and stiff.

4. Fold chocolate mixture into egg whites. Fold in whipped cream.

5. Spoon the filling mixture into Chocolate Crumb Crust and chill overnight.

Serves 8 to 10

CHOCOLATE CRUMB CRUST

1½ cups graham cracker crumbs	⅓ cup butter or margarine, melted
¼ cup brown sugar, packed	
one 1-ounce square unsweetened chocolate, melted	

1. Combine crumbs and sugar. Add melted chocolate and melted butter and blend thoroughly.

2. Pat mixture into a 9-inch pie plate and chill thoroughly before adding filling.

PICNIC NOTE: Due to the raw egg and cream content, *this pie must be kept thoroughly chilled prior to serving.* If taken on a summer picnic, do not allow it to sit in the sun. Return it to the picnic cooler after serving.

Picnic on Ice

When frost nips the air and the ice is solid underfoot, sling your skates across your back and carry along a hot picnic lunch to enjoy around a campfire built at the edge of the pond to warm cold fingers and toes and for roasting marinated hot dogs. If Skaters' Chocolate doesn't warm you up, Texas Chili certainly will. Eat it as a hot, thick soup from large mugs, or spoon it over the hot dogs in buns for the best chili dogs this side of the Rio Grande. Take along marshmallows for toasting if you like, but you're bound to be full after you try a fruit salad tossed with rice and Creamy Pear Dressing, a recipe you'll want to use again and again once you've tried it. After the last whirl around the ice, don't head home until everyone has tried the Cranberry Spice Cake, a wonderful winter treat for hungry skaters.

SKATERS' CHOCOLATE

This steamy beverage is sure to warm even the coldest skater. A special liqueur can be added at serving time so the "unadulterated" chocolate is available for the little skaters in the crowd and for the adults who prefer their chocolate straight.

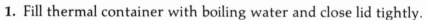

boiling water to fill a 10-cup thermal container	6½ cups milk
½ cup cocoa	miniature marshmallows
1 teaspoon salt	Chocolate-flavored brandy
one 14-ounce can sweetened condensed milk	or Vandermint liqueur (optional)

1. Fill thermal container with boiling water and close lid tightly.

2. In a 3-quart saucepan, combine cocoa and salt and stir in the condensed milk.

3. Over medium heat, slowly stir in the milk. Heat almost to boiling.

4. Empty thermal container of boiling water and immediately transfer hot chocolate to container. Cover tightly.

5. Carry marshmallows and selected liqueur to skating-picnic site. To serve, give chocolate a good stir. Add a shot of liqueur (if desired) and/or marshmallows to each cup of steamy chocolate and stir well.

Serves 6 to 8

STUFFED ONIONS

6   medium to large yellow onions, peeled
1   cup finely chopped boiled ham
1   cup fine bread crumbs
1   cup finely chopped fresh spinach, firmly packed
¼   cup butter or margarine, melted

1   egg, slightly beaten
¼   cup grated Parmesan cheese
1   teaspoon parsley flakes
1   teaspoon dried basil
⅛   teaspoon dried oregano
¼   teaspoon salt
⅛   teaspoon pepper

1. Parboil peeled onions for 10 minutes. Drain and plunge into cold water.

2. Preheat oven to 375°F.

3. Cut off pointed top of each onion and carefully cut out the center pulp of each onion, leaving a shell ½ to ¾ inch thick. Set shells aside to drain.

4. Chop removed pulp finely or put through the blender on the chop cycle. Mix chopped pulp with remaining ingredients.

5. Stuff onion shells with the ham mixture.

6. Place stuffed onions on a rack in a baking pan containing ¼ inch of water, or place each onion in a well-greased muffin tin. Bake 30 to 40 minutes, until well heated and tender.

7. Serve warm or well chilled.

Serves 6

PICNIC NOTE: Pack prepared onions close together in an airtight hard-sided container.

BACON-WRAPPED MARINATED HOT DOGS

8   hot dogs (1 pound)
½   cup dry red wine or apple
      juice
2   tablespoons vegetable oil
¼   cup lemon juice
1   clove garlic, minced
½   teaspoon salt
½   teaspoon crumbled dried
      rosemary

2   tablespoons ketchup
1   teaspoon Dijon-style
      mustard
1   tablespoon brown sugar
2   tablespoons finely minced
      onion
8   slices bacon

1. Score hot dogs diagonally. Place in a medium-size bowl.

2. Combine remaining ingredients except bacon strips in a small saucepan and mix thoroughly. Heat to boiling and pour over scored hot dogs. Allow to marinate at least 1 hour.

3. Skewer hot dogs. Wrap a slice of bacon diagonally around each hot dog and secure with water-soaked toothpicks.

4. Grill over hot coals, basting with marinade if desired.

5. Serve in hot dog buns or French rolls with favorite condiments or spoon Texas Chili (below) over them.

Serves 6 to 8

TEXAS CHILI

2 to 3   tablespoons olive oil
1   medium-size onion, chopped
1   clove garlic, minced
2   pounds lean ground beef
one   28-ounce can
        tomatoes, or 3½ cups
        peeled, seeded and
        chopped fresh
        tomatoes
one   15½-ounce can kidney
        beans (including
        canning liquid)

2 to 3   tablespoons chili
        powder (to your liking)
3   whole cloves
½   stick cinnamon
1   teaspoon ground coriander
½   teaspoon paprika
2   tablespoons brown sugar
salt and pepper to taste
½   cup brandy (optional)
corn chips (optional)

1. Heat oil in heavy skillet and sauté onion and garlic. Add beef and brown, stirring often to avoid lumps.

2. Add remaining ingredients except brandy, stir well to mix and simmer, uncovered, 2 to 3 hours. Adjust seasonings.

3. Stir in the brandy (if desired) and continue to simmer for 15 minutes. Just before serving or packing in a thermal container, remove the cloves and cinnamon stick.

4. Serve in large bowls or mugs or straight from wide-mouthed thermal containers. Garnish with corn chips, if desired. This chili is great over fire-roasted potatoes, too, or spooned over hot dogs in buns.

Serves 6 to 8

WINTER FRUIT SALAD

1 cup raw long-grain white rice, cooked according to package directions
¾ cup Creamy Pear Dressing (below)
½ cup sliced celery
½ cup chopped dates
½ cup coarsely chopped hazelnuts

2 medium-size ripe pears, peeled and diced
2 large tangerines or oranges, peeled, sectioned and chopped
¼ pound green or red grapes, halved and seeded

1. Combine rice, dressing, celery and dates in a large salad bowl. Toss until rice is well coated with dressing.

2. Chill until just before serving time. Fold in remaining ingredients. Add more dressing if desired.

3. To serve, arrange on lettuce leaves.

Serves 6 to 8

CREAMY PEAR DRESSING

1 large ripe pear, peeled, cored and cut into chunks
juice and grated rind of 1 lime
½ cup lemon juice
¼ cup honey

½ teaspoon celery seed
½ teaspoon salt
dash of white pepper
1 cup vegetable oil

1. Place all ingredients except oil in blender jar and purée.

2. With blender at medium speed, slowly pour oil into whirling purée and mix well. Pour into another jar, cover and refrigerate.

Yield: about 2 cups

CRANBERRY SPICE CAKE

1½ cups raw cranberries
½ cup butter or margarine, softened
1 cup brown sugar, packed
2 eggs
2 cups all-purpose flour, unsifted
2 teaspoons baking powder
1 teaspoon cinnamon

grated rind of 1 large orange
½ teaspoon baking soda
½ teaspoon salt
½ teaspoon ground cloves
½ cup apple cider or orange juice
1 teaspoon vanilla
4 ounces walnuts, chopped
1 recipe Orange Glaze (below)

1. Preheat oven to 350°F.

2. Sort and wash cranberries, then cut in half and place in medium-size mixing bowl.

3. Cream butter and sugar together in another medium-size mixing bowl. Add eggs, one at a time, and beat thoroughly after each addition.

4. Combine flour, baking powder, cinnamon, orange rind, soda, salt and cloves. Mix one-fourth of this flour mixture with the cut cranberries.

5. Beat remaining flour mixture into sugar and butter mixture in small portions alternately with the cider.

6. Stir in cranberry-flour mixture, vanilla and walnuts.

7. Turn batter into a greased and floured 10-cup tube pan or fluted cake pan. Bake for 50 minutes or until toothpick inserted in center comes out clean. Cool in pan 10 minutes, then invert onto rack and drizzle with Orange Glaze.

Serves 12

PICNIC NOTE: This is a dense, moist cake which travels well. If kept for a long period of time, it should be refrigerated to avoid spoiling.

ORANGE GLAZE

½ cup unsifted confectioners' sugar
1½ tablespoons orange juice

1 tablespoon butter, softened

1. In a small mixing bowl, cream ingredients together until smooth.

2. Drizzle over cake.

Yield: about ⅜ cup

Christmas Picnic Package

Instead of buying individual gifts for a special family on your Christmas list, pack an easy-to-fix breakfast meal in a pretty basket and deliver it on Christmas Eve with specific instructions to open before breakfast on Christmas morning. Weary parents will welcome a picnic hamper brimming with a scrumptious brunch designed to take the work out of Christmas morning.

Choose a sturdy picnic basket or hamper and line it with colorful Christmas tissue paper. Inside, place prepared foods in containers meant to be part of the total gift. Pack the Christmas waffle mix and the butter sauce for Steamed Cranberry Pudding in plastic containers with airtight lids, and tape the directions for final preparation to the lids. Friendship Fruit is especially pretty packed in an apothecary jar with a snug-fitting top. Tie a big bow around the bottle of maple syrup and pack the Honey Pecan Butter in a small crock or brightly colored plastic tub. Tuck in a can of English Breakfast or Earl Grey tea, a special coffee, and hot chocolate mix for the children. Then add a chunk of Jarlsberg cheese in airtight transparent wrap, and a tasty sausage. Tuck in copies of all the recipes, or, better yet, a copy of this book.

MENU

Champagne or Sparkling Water

Friendship Fruit*

Christmas Cinnamon Waffles*

Honey Pecan Butter*

Maple Syrup   Sausage

Jarlsberg Cheese

Steamed Cranberry Pudding*

Tea   Coffee   Hot Chocolate

FRIENDSHIP FRUIT

This variation of fresh fruit *rompertopf* (German for brandied fruit) allows you to make sweet brandied fruit all year long. Once started, it's a wonderful gift from the kitchen.

Starter

1 cup fresh fruit, peeled, pitted and sliced (plums, peaches, apricots, nectarines)

1 cup sugar
1 cup brandy

1. Sterilize a large glass jar in boiling water.

2. Add fresh fruit slices, sugar and brandy, and mix well. Cover with cheesecloth; store in a cool place overnight or a few days.

3. Stir in 1 cup of any of the canned fruits suggested below, including canning syrup, or add 1 cup of the frozen or dried fruits and 1 cup sugar. Cover and store as directed above.

4. Within the next week, repeat Steps 2 and 3 twice, each time adding a different fruit. After the last addition, cover the fruit with cheesecloth and store in a cool place for 2 to 4 weeks, until the

fruit is fermented to a sweet, brandied flavor. Be sure to stir the mixture thoroughly every 3 or 4 days during the storage period.

5. Cover the fermented fruit tightly and store in a cool place. Give starter cups to friends and continue to add your favorite canned fruits as you deplete your supply.

6. Serve as a sauce over waffles or pancakes, shortcake, ice cream or pound cake.

Yield: 4-cup starter batch

SUGGESTED FRUITS

Canned	Frozen	Dried
pineapple chunks	strawberries	apricots
sliced peaches	blueberries	prunes
maraschino cherries	raspberries	raisins
fruit cocktail	rhubarb	
pears (cut into chunks)		

CHRISTMAS CINNAMON WAFFLES

2	cups sifted all-purpose flour	1	teaspoon cinnamon
3	teaspoons baking powder	2	eggs, separated
1	teaspoon salt	1½	cups milk
2	tablespoons sugar	6	tablespoons salad oil

1. Sift dry ingredients together into medium-size bowl.

2. Beat the egg yolks, and stir in the milk and oil.

3. Pour egg yolk mixture into the dry ingredients and stir just enough to moisten.

4. Beat egg whites until stiff but not dry. Fold into waffle batter.

5. Grease a hot waffle iron and pour batter onto one surface to within 1 inch of the edge. Bake 4 to 5 minutes.

6. Serve with Honey Pecan Butter (page 177) or maple syrup, or spoon Friendship Fruit (page 175) over the top.

Yield: 6 waffles

PICNIC NOTE: To give this as a gift, complete Step 1, above, and place dry ingredients in a medium-size container with an airtight lid. Copy the remaining instructions onto a small card and tape the card to the lid of the container.

HONEY PECAN BUTTER

¾ cup honey   ½ cup finely chopped pecans
½ cup butter, softened

1. In a small mixing bowl, beat honey until white and fluffy. Gradually beat in the butter. Stir in the chopped pecans.

2. Spoon honey mixture into a small dish or butter crock.

Yield: 2 cups

STEAMED CRANBERRY PUDDING

¼ cup light or dark molasses   2 cups raw cranberry halves
¼ cup brown sugar, packed   1 teaspoon vanilla
⅓ cup water   pinch of salt
1⅓ cups all-purpose flour   Hot Butter Sauce (below)
2 teaspoons baking soda

1. Mix all ingredients except sauce together in the order listed.

2. Pour mixture into a well-greased 1-pound coffee can. Cover lightly with a square of aluminum foil and secure with a rubber band.

3. Place the filled can on a rack in a large pot with 2 inches of water and bring to a boil. Reduce heat and steam 1½ to 2 hours. A toothpick inserted in the center of the pudding should have moist but not sticky crumbs when removed.

4. Remove pudding from can and serve warm or cold in slices with Hot Butter Sauce.

Serves 6

HOT BUTTER SAUCE

1 cup sugar   ½ cup heavy cream
½ cup butter   1½ teaspoons vanilla

1. Mix ingredients together in a small saucepan, then bring to a boil.

2. Serve warm over Steamed Cranberry Pudding.

Yield: about 1½ cups

PICNIC NOTE: Wrap the pudding in foil with a note to reheat in the foil for 15 minutes in a hot oven. Prepare Hot Butter Sauce and pour it into an airtight container; attach a note to reheat over medium heat, stirring until the butter is melted and the ingredients are well blended.

Super Bowl Sunday Peasant Fare

MENU

Raclette* with Assorted Crackers

Black Bean Peasant Soup*

Mushroom Pilaf*

Yankee Spiced Beef*

Apple Corn Bread*

Popcorn with Parmesan Butter*

Brandied Nuts*

Beer   Hearty Burgundy Wine

Apricot-Date Flan*

Coffee   Tea

Whether your team is winning or losing, Super Bowl Sunday is a perfect time for a winter picnic around a crackling fire. Invite friends to share hearty peasant fare at your hearthside while they watch the game. Be sure to stock plenty of soda and beer, pretzels and peanuts for predinner snacking. To fill your home with a pleasant aroma, throw dried orange peels onto the fire. At serving time, arrange the food and eating utensils on or near the hearth where the Raclette is melting to spread on crackers as an appetizer for what's to come.

RACLETTE

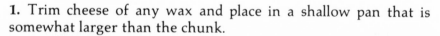

This is a simple but delicious appetizer for a wintry fireside picnic where guests help themselves to a Swiss peasant cheese dish.

2-pound   chunk of any of
          the following mellow
          cheeses, or a
          combination of them
          in smaller chunks:

          Swiss
          Gruyère
          Jack
          Muenster
          Kasseri

Melba toast
crackers
small rounds of rye bread
   or Pita Bread (page 159),
   cut into pieces
a warm, glowing fire

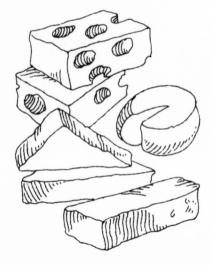

1. Trim cheese of any wax and place in a shallow pan that is somewhat larger than the chunk.

2. Set the pan on the hearth and push the widest surface of the cheese close to the fire.

3. When the face of the cheese begins to melt, scrape it off and spoon onto toast, crackers, or bread. If you're using Kasseri cheese, sprinkle with a little lemon juice once the melted cheese is spread on bread.

Serves 6 to 8 as an appetizer

PICNIC NOTE: Each cheese tastes slightly different when melted by the fire, so it's nice to use several cheeses instead of only one. If you wish to serve Raclette in its most traditional manner, include baby pickles and small boiled potatoes in the menu.

BLACK BEAN PEASANT SOUP

3 cups dried black beans
1 pound bacon
1 large onion, chopped
2 cloves garlic, finely minced
1 large firm tomato, peeled, seeded and finely chopped
pinch of freshly ground pepper
¼ teaspoon ground coriander

¼ teaspoon dried thyme
¼ teaspoon ground marjoram
1 bay leaf
4 cups beef or chicken broth
2 cups water
½ cup dark rum (optional)
grated Parmesan cheese
fresh parsley sprigs

1. Place beans in a large bowl and cover with cold water. Soak overnight. Drain and set aside.

2. Fry bacon until crisp. Drain, crumble and refrigerate.

3. Measure 6 tablespoons of the bacon drippings into a 5-quart heavy saucepan. Add onion and garlic and cook 5 minutes, until tender.

4. Stir in tomato, pepper, coriander, thyme, marjoram and bay leaf. Add broth, 2 cups water and beans. Bring to a boil, then reduce heat, cover tightly and simmer for 3 to 4 hours. Adjust seasonings after soup has simmered for an hour, adding salt if necessary.

5. Cool soup slightly. Purée in blender in small batches, but do not purée too finely. Soup should be slightly chunky. Return soup purée to saucepan.

6. Add rum (if desired) then heat the soup, but do not boil. Adjust seasonings if necessary.

7. Serve in bowls or mugs or over pilaf. Sprinkle with crumbled bacon and Parmesan cheese, and garnish with parsley sprigs.

Serves 6 to 8

MUSHROOM PILAF

4 tablespoons butter or margarine	one 10½-ounce can beef consommé
1 small onion, finely chopped	1 cup Chablis wine or water
¼ pound fresh mushrooms, finely chopped	½ teaspoon salt
	dash of pepper
1 clove garlic, minced	1 teaspoon dried basil
1 cup raw long-grain white rice	½ cup pine nuts or slivered almonds
¼ cup raisins	

1. Preheat oven to 350°F.

2. Melt butter in a heavy, high-sided skillet. Add onion, mushrooms and garlic, and cook over medium heat until the onion is soft but not browned.

3. Stir in the rice and heat a few minutes. Then add remaining ingredients except pine nuts and bring to a boil.

4. Transfer rice mixture to a casserole and cover. Bake for 45 minutes to 1 hour, until the liquid is absorbed and the rice is cooked through. Stir occasionally during the baking period.

5. Stir in pine nuts just before serving.

Serves 6

YANKEE SPICED BEEF

2 beef bouillon cubes	2 teaspoons Constant Comment loose tea
1 cup boiling water	
3 sticks cinnamon	one 16-ounce can whole cranberry sauce
8 whole cloves	
8 peppercorns	4-pound lean beef brisket

1. Preheat oven to 275°F.

2. In a deep roaster pan large enough to accommodate the beef brisket, dissolve bouillon cubes in the boiling water.

3. Crush cinnamon, cloves and peppercorns, or whirl in the blender. Add tea.

4. Mix spices and tea with the cranberry sauce and coat the beef brisket with the mixture.

5. Place coated meat in the dissolved bouillon. Weight meat with a heavy object like a brick wrapped in aluminum foil. Cover roaster and bake for 3½ hours. Let cool, then scrape off cranberry sauce.

Wipe meat with a damp cloth and wrap in foil. Refrigerate, weighted with brick, for at least 2 days.

6. To serve, slice thinly for sandwiches or arrange on a serving platter and serve with cold or hot Brandied Cranberry Sauce (page 113) or with prepared horseradish.

Serves 6 to 8

APPLE CORN BREAD

1 cup coarsely grated, peeled raw apple	1 tablespoon honey
1 cup yellow cornmeal	¾ cup boiling water
1 teaspoon cinnamon	2 eggs, separated
2 tablespoons vegetable oil	2 tablespoons cold water

1. Preheat oven to 400°F.

2. Combine apple, cornmeal, cinnamon, vegetable oil and honey in a mixing bowl. Stir in boiling water.

3. In a small bowl, combine egg yolks and cold water. Beat together, then stir into cornmeal mixture.

4. Beat egg whites until stiff but not dry, then fold into the cornmeal batter.

5. Pour batter into a greased 9-inch square baking pan and bake for 25 to 30 minutes, until lightly browned and toothpick inserted in center comes out clean.

6. Cut into 9 squares and serve the bread piping hot or at room temperature.

Yield: 9 pieces

PARMESAN BUTTER

1 cup butter	1 teaspoon dried oregano
2 cups freshly grated Parmesan cheese	1 teaspoon dried basil

1. Cream all ingredients together, pack in a crock or tub, cover and refrigerate.

2. Serve over hot, popped popcorn.

Yield: about 1½ cups

BRANDIED NUTS

These make tasty snacks for all kinds of picnics.

¼ cup butter	1 cup pecan halves
2¼ cups confectioners' sugar	1 cup blanched almonds
¼ cup brandy, or ¼ teaspoon imitation brandy flavoring plus ¼ cup water	

1. Preheat oven to 350°F.

2. Cream butter and work in sugar and brandy.

3. Spread nuts on a baking sheet and toast in the oven until nuts are golden.

4. While nuts are hot, stir them into the sugar mixture and, when well coated, spread them on waxed paper to cool.

Yield: 2 cups

APRICOT-DATE FLAN

3 eggs	pinch of salt
⅓ cup sugar	1 cup finely chopped dried apricots
⅓ cup all-purpose flour	
2 cups milk	½ cup finely chopped dates
1 cup light cream	1 cup apricot jam, melted (optional)
½ cup slivered almonds	

1. Preheat oven to 350°F.

2. Mix eggs and sugar together and beat to form a ribbon. Then add flour and stir carefully to avoid lumps. Add milk and cream and mix to form a smooth paste.

3. Whirl almonds in the blender to pulverize, then add to milk and egg mixture. Stir in salt, apricots and dates, and mix well.

4. Pour mixture into an oiled ovenproof 10-cup dish or mold and bake for 20 minutes or until knife inserted in the center comes out clean. Remove from oven, allow to cool, then refrigerate.

5. To unmold, run a knife between the custard and the mold, then place a serving dish upside down over the custard and invert quickly.

6. Glaze with melted apricot jam if desired.

Serves 6

Winter Ski Picnic

Join friends for a day on the slopes in the crisp mountain air or on a cross-country trek in wide-open snowfields highlighted by a picnic lunch spread off the trail—or at hearthside. There's nothing better to assuage fresh-air appetites than a cup of hot steamy soup from a thermos. Follow Herbed Mushroom Soup with a tasty sandwich loaf, a new variation on turkey salad, and crunchy green beans in a buttermilk dressing. Large chunks of chocolate pound cake accompanied by fruit and cheese will provide a new spurt of energy to complete the day's activities in fine form.

If you take along a small thermos of hot maple syrup, later in the afternoon you can enjoy Sugar-On-Snow, a New England treat savored during maple sugar time. Drizzle the hot syrup on *clean* snow and let it harden to sticky taffy in the cold air, then scoop it up and enjoy!

MENU

Herbed Mushroom Soup*

Turkey Salad Macadamia*

Shrimp and Spinach Wheels*

Green Beans and Prosciutto with Almonds*

Grapes   **Gruyère Cheese**   Apples

Chocolate Cream Cheese Pound Cake*

Hot Buttered Cranberry Cocktail*
(page 198)

Sugar-On-Snow

HERBED MUSHROOM SOUP

4 tablespoons butter or margarine	dash of cayenne pepper
1½ pounds fresh mushrooms, sliced	salt and pepper to taste
	¼ cup sherry or water
3 medium-size onions, sliced	two 10¾-ounce cans chicken broth
1 clove garlic, minced	2 egg yolks
1 teaspoon dried basil	1 cup light cream
1 teaspoon dried oregano	freshly grated mozzarella or Parmesan cheese
¼ teaspoon dried thyme	

1. Melt butter in a large heavy saucepan and sauté mushrooms, onions and garlic. Add seasonings and sherry and cook 5 to 10 minutes over medium heat. Add chicken broth and bring to a boil. Reduce heat, cover and simmer for 45 minutes.

2. Purée vegetable mixture, including cooking liquid, in blender. Return to saucepan.

3. Beat egg yolks and cream together, then stir in a little of the purée. Add egg mixture to the purée in the saucepan, mix well and heat, but do not boil.

4. Serve hot, sprinkled with freshly grated mozzarella or Parmesan cheese.

Yield: 5 to 6 cups

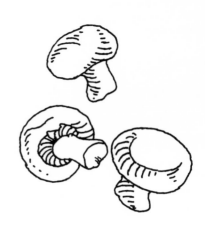

TURKEY SALAD MACADAMIA

2   cups diced cooked turkey (or chicken)
4   stalks celery, finely sliced
3   scallions, finely sliced (including part of the green tops)
½ to 1   cup coarsely chopped macadamia nuts
½   cup chopped dates
1   cup halved seedless green grapes
½   cup plain yogurt
½   cup dairy sour cream
2   tablespoons orange juice
1   tablespoon grated orange rind
2   teaspoons Dijon-style mustard
½   teaspoon salt
dash of white pepper
crisp lettuce leaves
1   orange, thinly sliced

1. Combine turkey with celery, scallions, nuts, dates and grapes in a medium-size bowl.

2. Blend yogurt, sour cream, orange juice and rind, mustard, salt and pepper, and fold into turkey mixture. Cover and chill.

3. Serve scooped onto lettuce leaves. Garnish with orange slices.

Serves 6

Variation: You can easily extend this salad with cooked pasta—try shell macaroni. For each 8 ounces of uncooked macaroni add ¼ to ½ cup dressing.

SHRIMP AND SPINACH WHEELS

two   8-ounce loaves French or Italian bread
1   egg
½   cup dry white wine or chicken broth
1   medium-size onion, finely chopped
¼   cup chopped fresh basil, or 2 tablespoons dried basil
1   teaspoon olive oil
½   cup finely shredded Swiss cheese
2   tablespoons butter or margarine
1   large clove garlic, minced
¼   pound fresh mushrooms, wiped clean and finely chopped
1½   pounds shrimp, cooked, shelled, cleaned and cut into small chunks
one   10-ounce package frozen chopped spinach, or 1 pound fresh spinach, chopped
⅛   teaspoon nutmeg
salt and pepper to taste

1. Preheat oven to 400°F.

2. Prepare bread by cutting a lengthwise slit in the underside of each loaf. Carefully remove bread inside, leaving crust shell intact. Break up bread chunks and place in a mixing bowl.

3. Beat egg with wine and pour over bread in mixing bowl. Let stand 5 minutes. Squeeze any excess liquid from the bread. Add onion, basil, oil and cheese, and mix well. Set aside.

4. Melt butter in a heavy skillet. Add garlic, mushrooms and shrimp, and sauté 4 to 5 minutes over medium heat. Stir in spinach, nutmeg and salt and pepper to taste. Raise heat and cook, stirring occasionally, about 5 minutes, until almost all the cooking liquid is absorbed.

5. Add shrimp-spinach mixture to bread mixture and mix thoroughly. Squeeze out excess moisture.

6. Pack loaves with prepared mixture and bring the bottom edges together. Wrap the stuffed loaves in foil and bake for 30 minutes or until heated through. Allow to cool slightly.

7. Slice and serve warm, or refrigerate and slice and serve cold.

Serves 8 to 12

GREEN BEANS AND PROSCIUTTO WITH ALMONDS

½ pound fresh green beans, or one 10-ounce package frozen green beans	¼ pound thinly sliced prosciutto
	¼ pound Swiss cheese
1 quart salad greens (romaine, watercress, Boston lettuce)	Buttermilk Dressing (below)
	⅓ cup slivered almonds

1. Cook green beans in salted water until cooked through but still crisp. Plunge into cold water to stop cooking action. Drain.

2. Wash, pat dry and tear salad greens into bite-size pieces. Place in a salad bowl lined with additional greens.

3. Cut prosciutto and cheese into matchstick pieces and add to salad greens. Add drained green beans to salad and toss ingredients lightly.

4. At serving time, pour dressing over the salad, toss to coat and sprinkle with almonds.

Serves 6

Variations: Substitute Creamy Pear Dressing (page 173) or Vinaigrette Dressing (page 190) for Buttermilk Dressing.

BUTTERMILK DRESSING
½   cup buttermilk
½   clove garlic, minced
¼   teaspoon sugar
¼   teaspoon dry mustard
¼   teaspoon salt
fresh ground pepper to taste

1. Combine ingredients in a shaker jar.

2. Shake vigorously to mix.

CHOCOLATE CREAM CHEESE POUND CAKE

1   cup margarine
½   cup butter
one   8-ounce package cream cheese
2   cups sugar
1   cup dark brown sugar, packed

½   cup unsweetened cocoa
6   eggs
2½   cups sifted all-purpose flour
1   tablespoon vanilla

1. Preheat oven to 325°F.

2. In a very large bowl, cream margarine, butter and cream cheese together until light and fluffy. Place the bowl in the sink to avoid spattering batter all over the kitchen.

3. Add sugars and cocoa to creamed mixture and blend well.

4. Add 2 of the eggs, beat well, then add 1 cup of the flour and beat well. Repeat with remaining eggs and flour, ending with ½ cup flour. Beat well after each addition. Add vanilla and mix well.

5. Grease a 10-inch tube pan and dust it with cocoa.

6. Spoon cake batter into prepared tube pan. Bake for 1 hour and 25 minutes, until toothpick inserted in center comes out clean. ABSOLUTELY NO PEEKING during baking period. Allow cake to cool in pan for 10 minutes, then invert pan and remove cake to wire rack. Allow to cool.

7. Serve plain or with a dollop of whipped cream and a sprinkling of grated orange rind.

Serves 10 to 20

PICNIC NOTE: Cover the cake loosely with foil to transport it. This cake is quite firm and travels well cut into pieces and individually wrapped for hikers or bikers.

MORE GOOD FOOD TO GO

The Basics

Included in this brief chapter are recipes for basics—foods or ingredients that occur regularly in the recipes and menus throughout this book. I have tried to keep all recipes in the book as simple as possible, often using frozen vegetables and dried herbs in place of fresh, and canned chicken and beef stocks in place of homemade. Needless to say, fresh or homemade ingredients can and should be substituted as time and budget permit for even tastier results. In fact, I heartily recommend it!

There are two ingredients on which I *never* compromise—pastry and mayonnaise. Recipes for both are included here. However, packaged pie crust mix can be substituted when time is of the essence, and commercially prepared mayonnaise (not salad dressing) is an acceptable alternative for fresh.

In substituting fresh herbs for dried, use twice the amount. For example, substitute 2 tablespoons of fresh snipped parsley when a recipe calls for 1 tablespoon of parsley flakes.

Basic recipes for standard picnic drinks, seasoned butters for sandwich breads, basic salad dressings and meat marinades are also included here, as well as a brief discussion on choosing, packing and serving picnic wines.

PASTRY

The secret to flaky pastry is the use of ice water and as little working of the dough as possible. I love a buttery crust so I always use unsalted butter, but margarine or shortening is also acceptable. If you use salted butter or margarine, you might want to reduce the amount of salt slightly.

Single Crust	Double Crust
(for 8- or 9-inch one-crust pie)	(for 8- or 9-inch two-crust pie)
1 cup sifted all-purpose flour	2 cups sifted all-purpose flour
½ teaspoon salt	¾ teaspoon salt
⅓ cup sweet butter or margarine	⅔ cup sweet butter or margarine
2 to 3 tablespoons ice water	4 to 6 tablespoons ice water

1. Combine flour and salt in mixing bowl.

2. With a pastry blender, cut in half the butter and work until the mixture resembles fine meal.

3. Cut in remaining butter and work until mixture resembles small peas.

4. Sprinkle with the minimum amount of ice water and work in quickly with pastry blender or fork. *Add only enough water to hold the mixture together and do not overwork.*

5. Form dough into a ball (two of about equal size for double crust) and roll out on a floured surface, fit into pie plate and bake as directed in specific recipes throughout this book.

RICH PASTRY

3¾ cups sifted all-purpose flour	⅓ cup shortening
½ teaspoon baking powder	1 egg yolk, beaten
1½ teaspoons salt	about ½ cup ice water
1¼ cups butter or margarine	

1. Combine flour with baking powder and salt in a medium-size mixing bowl.

2. With a pastry blender, cut in butter and shortening until mixture resembles coarse meal.

3. Add the beaten egg yolk and just enough ice water to hold dough together without crumbling. Work in quickly with pastry blender or fork. *Do not overwork.*

4. Round up dough and use as directed in recipes calling for this pastry.

MAYONNAISE

2 egg yolks	¼ cup lemon juice
1 teaspoon dry mustard	1 cup olive oil
½ teaspoon salt	1 cup salad oil
pinch of cayenne pepper	

1. Beat egg yolks until thick and lemon colored. Add seasonings and half of the lemon juice. Beat well.

2. Mix oils together and add to egg yolk mixture drop by drop, beating continuously. Gradually increase the amount of oil added as the mixture thickens.

3. Slowly add remaining lemon juice and beat well. Cover and chill at least 1 hour before using.

Yield: about 2½ cups

MUSTARD MAYONNAISE

2 egg yolks	1 teaspoon Dijon-style mustard
1 tablespoon lemon juice	dash of pepper
1 tablespoon red wine vinegar	½ cup salad oil
½ teaspoon salt	

1. Place all ingredients except oil in blender jar and mix well.

2. With motor running, slowly pour in the oil to make a thick sauce.

3. Turn into a small bowl, cover and chill.

Yield: ¾ cup

PICNIC NOTE: Keep chilled until serving time.

VINAIGRETTE DRESSING

½ cup olive oil	1½ teaspoons salt
1½ tablespoons red wine vinegar	1½ teaspoons lemon juice
1½ teaspoons Dijon-style mustard	½ teaspoon confectioners' sugar

1. Combine ingredients in a shaker jar and shake vigorously to combine.

2. Serve over mixed greens.

Yield: ½ cup

YOGURT-SOUR CREAM DRESSING

½ cup plain yogurt   ½ cup dairy sour cream

1. Mix together in a small bowl.

2. Serve as a salad dressing with vegetables or fruit or as a dip for raw vegetables. This is especially nice for artichoke-dipping in place of melted butter or mayonnaise.

Variation: Add ¼ to 1 teaspoon of one of your favorite dried herbs—chives, dill, tarragon, rosemary—for a more flavorful version.

Yield: 1 cup

BEEF TERIYAKI MARINADE

¼ cup brown sugar, packed   1 tablespoon salad oil
¼ cup soy sauce   ¼ teaspoon ground ginger
2 tablespoons lemon juice   1 clove garlic, minced

1. Combine all ingredients in a small bowl and mix well.

2. Spoon marinade over meat and refrigerate. Allow to marinate 2 to 6 hours or overnight. Turn and baste meat occasionally.

Yield: about ½ cup

Variation: Try this marinade on chicken and fish, too.

SHISH KEBAB MARINADE

¼ cup red wine   ½ teaspoon pepper
¼ cup salad oil   1 tablespoon prepared
1 tablespoon cider vinegar   mustard
1 teaspoon onion salt   1 bay leaf
1 teaspoon celery salt   2 tablespoons chopped
¾ teaspoon garlic salt, or 1   fresh parsley, or 2
     clove garlic, minced   teaspoons parsley
½ teaspoon salt   flakes
1 teaspoon dried oregano

1. Combine all ingredients in a small saucepan and mix thoroughly. Heat to boiling, remove from heat and allow to cool.

2. Pour over meat, cover and refrigerate. Marinate several hours or overnight, turning and basting occasionally.

Yield: ½ cup

BLACK BRANDIED BARBECUE SAUCE

½ cup butter or margarine, melted
1 cup strong black coffee
one 5-ounce bottle Worcestershire sauce
½ cup brandy, or ¼ teaspoon imitation brandy flavoring plus ½ cup water

one 6-ounce can tomato paste
¼ cup lemon juice
2 tablespoons honey
1 teaspoon salt
1 teaspoon ground cloves

1. Combine all ingredients in a medium-size saucepan and mix well.

2. Bring to a boil, lower heat and simmer 30 minutes, stirring occasionally.

Yield: 3½ cups

BUTTERSCOTCH SAUCE

6 tablespoons butter or margarine
½ cup light brown sugar, packed
½ cup light honey

½ cup heavy cream
1 tablespoon plus 2 teaspoons lemon juice
slivered almonds or toasted hazelnuts

1. Melt butter in a small saucepan over medium heat. Stir in sugar and honey and mix well. Do not allow mixture to burn.

2. Add cream and cook over medium heat, stirring occasionally, until mixture comes to a boil and thickens. Remove from heat and stir in lemon juice.

3. Serve hot or cold over Irene's Vanilla Ice Cream (page 82) with a handful of slivered almonds or toasted hazelnuts.

Yield: about 1½ cups

RHUBARB SAUCE

2 cups diced fresh or frozen rhubarb	¼ teaspoon ground cloves
1 cup brown sugar, packed	¼ teaspoon nutmeg
½ teaspoon cinnamon	2 teaspoons grated orange rind

1. Preheat oven to 375°F.

2. Combine ingredients in a baking dish and bake until rhubarb is tender, about 1 hour.

3. Serve hot or cold over pound cake or ice cream, or chilled and stirred into plain yogurt.

Yield: about 2 cups

MAPLE CREAM FROSTING

4 tablespoons butter or margarine	1 tablespoon maple syrup
one 3-ounce package cream cheese	½ cup brown sugar, firmly packed
⅛ teaspoon salt	1½ cups confectioners' sugar

1. Cream butter and cream cheese together.

2. Add remaining ingredients and mix together until smooth. Add more confectioners' sugar if frosting is too moist to spread smoothly.

Yield: about 2¼ cups

CHOCOLATE CREAM FROSTING

4 tablespoons butter or margarine	1 teaspoon grated orange peel (optional)
4 ounces cream cheese	½ cup cocoa
⅛ teaspoon salt	1½ cups confectioners' sugar
2 teaspoons vanilla	

1. Cream butter and cream cheese together until fluffy.

2. Add remaining ingredients and mix together until smooth. Add more confectioners' sugar if frosting is too moist to spread smoothly.

Yield: about 2¼ cups

HERB BUTTERS

These two herb butters can be used in several ways with picnic foods. They add zest to sandwiches and are mouthwatering on heated breads.

To make Herb Buttered Bread, cut slices about three-quarters of the way through a loaf of French or Italian bread, then spread an herb butter on each slice, wrap the loaf in foil and bake it at 375°F for 15 to 20 minutes, until the butter has melted into the slices. Check the interior slices to be sure the entire loaf is done. This method can also be used for any presliced loaf; simply assemble the buttered slices in a loaf shape, wrap and bake. Slices can also be arranged, loaf-style in a bread pan, then covered with foil and baked as above. Carry hot loaves to the picnic wrapped in aluminum foil and several layers of newspaper to keep them warm until serving time.

These butters are also especially good on hot vegetables including potatoes and sweet corn, on beef or chicken, or on charcoal-grilled steaks. Try them on hot popcorn, too.

ITALIAN HERB BUTTER

½ cup butter or margarine	½ teaspoon powdered sage
½ teaspoon crumbled dried oregano	½ teaspoon salt
	¼ teaspoon pepper
1 teaspoon crumbled dried basil	¼ teaspoon garlic powder

1. Cream butter until fluffy.

2. Add herbs and mix well. Pack into a crock or tub, cover tightly and chill.

Yield: ½ cup

FRENCH HERB BUTTER

½ cup butter or margarine	½ teaspoon crumbled dried rosemary
1 teaspoon crumbled dried tarragon	½ teaspoon ground celery seed
½ teaspoon dried chervil	salt and pepper to taste
½ teaspoon powdered sage	
½ teaspoon crumbled dried thyme	

1. Cream butter until fluffy.

2. Add herbs and mix well. Pack into a crock or tub, cover tightly and chill.

Yield: ½ cup

SANDWICH BUTTER

This tasty butter mixture adds a little zest to otherwise ordinary sandwiches.

½	cup butter or margarine	1	teaspoon finely minced
½	teaspoon dry mustard		fresh parsley, or ½
½	teaspoon grated onion		teaspoon parsley
¼	teaspoon paprika		flakes

1. Cream all ingredients together and store, covered, in the refrigerator until ready to use.

2. Spread on bread for sandwiches.

Yield: ½ cup

SHALLOT BUTTER

½	pound shallots	½	pound butter, melted

1. Chop shallots, place in a wire strainer and pour boiling water over them.

2. Place shallots and melted butter in blender and purée.

3. Serve hot on vegetables or meat, or pour into a small crock or tub and chill. Use on broiled steak or fish or as a butter for sandwich-making.

Yield: about 1¼ cups

BEAN AND ALFALFA SPROUTS

Bean and alfalfa sprouts make tasty, crunchy additions to salads and sandwiches. They are finding their way into more and more grocery stores, especially those that carry gourmet foods. However, you can "grow" them following the directions below.

1. Prepare a 1-quart jar with a wide mouth and a lid. With a nail or ice pick, carefully punch holes in the lid of the jar, or cut a piece of wire screen slightly larger than the ring for a standard quart jar and force the screen into the ring.

2. Measure ¼ to ⅓ cup mung beans or soybeans or 2 to 3 tablespoons alfalfa seed into prepared jar. Cover with water. Soak overnight in a dark place.

3. In the morning, drain off the water. Then shake the beans onto the side of the jar and place the jar on its side in a cupboard that you open frequently.

4. Each day, rinse the beans at least twice and watch them grow. In about 4 days the bean sprouts will be over 1 inch long and ready to use. Alfalfa sprouts might be ready sooner. Drain water from sprouts and refrigerate any sprouts that you will not use immediately. They will keep for several days in the refrigerator.

CRUDITES

Crudité is the French term for crisp raw vegetables served as appetizers. Besides the crunchy carrots and celery sticks that turn up as standard picnic fare, most vegetables we normally serve hot are just as delicious—and sometimes better—when served raw with tasty vegetable and herb dips and sauces. While there is a wide variety of ways to decoratively prepare raw vegetables, nothing is more appealing than glistening fresh vegetables heaped in a large bowl ready for picnickers to help themselves. Consider including any or all of the vegetables listed, depending of course on seasonal availability. With few exceptions, the only preparation necessary for most is thorough cleansing, then packing on ice until the appointed hour for picnic feasting. If you're handy with the garnishing knife, of course, you can turn many of these into artful morsels—radish roses, carrot curls, scallion flowers, to name a few.

broccoli (flowerets or the whole head)	To slightly soften these vegetables, blanch them by plunging a few
cauliflower (flowerets or the whole head)	minutes into boiling water, then rinse quickly with ice
green beans	cold water.
red radishes	
cherry tomatoes	
whole fresh mushrooms	
scallions	
small white onions	Clean these vegetables thoroughly and
carrots	pack on ice.
celery	
zucchini	
yellow summer squash	
cucumbers	

NEVER FAIL ICED TEA

A friend swears this makes perfect iced tea. I have to agree. Just don't forget to mix it the night before the anticipated outing.

5 teaspoons of your favorite loose tea	4 cups cold water honey or sugar to taste

1. Mix tea and water together in a glass quart container, cover and let stand overnight.

2. Strain. Add honey or sugar to taste. Transfer to prechilled thermal container.

3. Serve over crushed ice. Garnish with fresh mint or lemon slices if desired.

Yield: 1 quart

HOMEMADE LEMONADE

If you prefer the "real thing" to frozen concentrate, use the following proportions for fresh lemonade. Double or triple as necessary.

6 large lemons	ice cubes
1 cup sugar	nutmeg
6 cups water	

1. Cut 2 of the lemons into ¼-inch-thick slices. Place in a thermal container with ½ cup of the sugar and press with a potato masher. Allow to stand for 15 minutes.

2. Meanwhile, place remaining 4 lemons in boiling water for 5 minutes. Remove and, when cool enough to handle, cut in half and squeeze out the juice. Add with water and remaining ½ cup sugar to the lemon-sugar mixture in the thermal container. Stir to mix well and dissolve sugar.

3. Add ice. Sprinkle with a little nutmeg to bring out the lemon flavor.

4. Servings can be garnished with sprigs of fresh mint.

Yield: 6 to 8 servings

STRAWBERRY PICNIC PUNCH

three 6-ounce cans frozen pink lemonade concentrate	½ cup sugar
	1 quart chilled ginger ale
one 10-ounce package frozen strawberries, thawed	fresh mint leaves

1. Dilute lemonade in a 1½-gallon jug according to the package directions.

2. Stir in thawed strawberries and sugar, and chill.

3. Just before serving, add ginger ale and mix well.

4. Serve over crushed ice and garnish with fresh mint leaves.

Yield: 1½ gallons

Variation: For an alcoholic version, omit the sugar and ginger ale. Add 1 bottle of chilled dry white dinner wine and ⅓ cup brandy to the thawed strawberries. Mix well.

HOT SPICED COFFEE

1 teaspoon finely chopped crystallized ginger	½ teaspoon nutmeg
	2 to 4 teaspoons honey
1 teaspoon grated orange rind	1 quart hot coffee

1. Combine spices and honey and stir into hot coffee.

2. To serve, pour into cups or mugs. Add more honey to suit individual tastes.

Yield: 4 cups

Variations: Prepare as above, then chill and serve over cracked ice. For an alcoholic version, add a shot of brandy or bourbon to each cup.

HOT BUTTERED CRANBERRY COCKTAIL

1½ quarts cranberry or cranberry-apple cocktail	¼ teaspoon crushed coriander seed
1 orange (with peel), sliced	butter pats
½ cup honey	

1. Place all ingredients except butter in a large saucepan and bring to boil. Simmer 15 minutes.

2. Ladle hot juice into cups or glasses and float a small pat of butter on top.

Yield: 6 cups

PICNIC NOTE: Carry this in a heated thermal container. Pack butter pats in a small plastic container to add at serving time. If you wish, carry along a bottle of your favorite wine—Burgundy, rosé or white—to mix in equal parts with the cocktail.

WINES FOR PICNICKING

For many picnickers, the picnic hamper or backpack is not complete without a bottle or a jug of their favorite wine whether the outing is a lazy summer day at the beach or dinner on a snowy hillside after a long trek on cross-country skis. The wine you choose need not be expensive to be enjoyed. For large groups of picnickers, you might want to purchase a good jug wine; they're available in a wide variety at purse-pleasing prices. Of course, for those intimate picnics for two, you might want to splurge on a really special spirit in a fifth or full quart or liter size.

Most wine experts agree that the best wines for picnic wining and dining include crisp whites, pink rosés and fruity reds, with full-bodied reds for the really hearty meals and champagne reserved for truly festive picnic occasions. French brut champagnes are a unanimous choice.

The following list is only a suggestion. Many other wines are equally well suited for picnic fare. My best advice is to choose something affordable you know you and your guests will enjoy. Consider including a choice from each of the three categories if the group is large and preferences vary.

Whites	**Pinks**
Chablis	Grenache Rosé
Chenin Blanc	Navalle Rosé
Graves (dry Bordeaux)	Pink Chablis
Johannesberg Riesling	
Liebfraumilch	**Reds**
Mountain White	Cabernet Sauvignon
Muscadet	Gamay Beaujolais
Pinot Chardonnay (inexpensive varieties)	Hearty Burgundy
Pouilly-Fumé (can be expensive)	Mountain Red
	Pinot Noir (inexpensive varieties)
	Zinfandel

Packing and Serving Tips

1. Whites, rosés and fruity red wines as well as champagne are usually served cold. Chill these for 2 hours in the refrigerator before packing the picnic. Never chill wine in the freezer.

2. Open all red wines 30 minutes before pouring to allow the wine to breathe.

3. Carry picnic wine in a specially designed wineskin (see page 15) to carry around your neck for skiing and hiking picnics.

4. Pack chilled wine in bottles in a thermal picnic hamper and stuff tissue paper around and between the bottles to prevent shaking and breaking. Handle with care. It's also a good idea to use extra refrigerants like the gels discussed on page 17 to keep the temperature constant in the cooler.

5. Don't forget to pack the corkscrew and, for special picnics, a wine carafe or decanter.

6. Wine can also be chilled at the picnic site by submerging the bottle(s) in a bucket filled with half ice, half water and allowing the bottle to stand for 30 minutes. A snowbank is a wonderful place for quick chilling; this method takes only a few minutes.

7. For Wine Spritzers, pour a few ounces of your favorite wine into a glass, then add ice cubes and fill with club soda for a refreshing cooler.

8. On a wintry day, serve wine half and half with any one of the hot fruit juice mixtures in this book. Add a pat of butter for hot buttered wine punch.

Mix and Match Recipes

Here you will find a little of everything as this chapter contains recipes that didn't quite fit into the picnic menus but are too good to omit. You can use them to make substitutions in the menus or to expand them when your picnics begin to snowball. Instead of increasing each of the recipes in a menu to meet the demands of a growing guest list, I simply add another dish or two and everyone shares, tasting a little of everything, Chinese-style.

ICED TOMATO VEGETABLE SOUP

3 large ripe tomatoes, peeled and finely chopped
2 medium-size cucumbers, peeled and finely chopped
1 medium-size onion, minced
1 large green pepper, seeded and finely chopped
1 large carrot, peeled and finely chopped
1 medium-size zucchini, chopped
½ cup chopped fresh parsley
1 to 2 Jalapeño peppers, seeded and chopped
1 clove garlic, minced
2 cups tomato or tomato-vegetable juice
2 tablespoons red wine vinegar
2 tablespoons olive oil
2 teaspoons salt
½ teaspoon pepper
grated rind of 1 lemon
ice cubes
fresh parsley sprigs

1. Place all ingredients in a large glass bowl and toss gently. Cover and store in refrigerator for several hours or overnight, until flavors have blended.

2. Garnish each serving with an ice cube and a sprig of parsley.

Yield: 7 to 8 cups

BEAN AND BACON BAKE

4 large potatoes, peeled and parboiled
½ cup butter or margarine, melted
1 large onion, sliced
4 firm tomatoes, sliced
two 15-ounce cans kidney beans

salt and pepper to taste
1 cup shredded Cheddar or mozzarella cheese
12 slices bacon, crisply fried, drained and coarsely crumbled

1. Cut a large sheet of heavy-duty aluminum foil or six to eight smaller pieces (about 8 inches square) for individual servings.

2. Slice potatoes and dip slices in melted butter to coat. Place in foil, dividing evenly among squares if you are preparing individual portions.

3. Add onion and tomato slices and kidney beans with some of the canning liquid. Add salt and pepper to taste. Sprinkle with cheese and bacon.

4. Seal foil packet(s) well (see page 34).

5. Place packet(s) on a grill over slow coals for 30 minutes, turning several times.

Serves 6 to 8

PICNIC NOTE: These ingredients can be layered in a casserole dish and baked at 350°F for 1 hour, or they can be prepared in a slow-cooker on low for 10 to 12 hours. Transfer the contents to a wide-mouthed thermal container or wrap the casserole in several layers of newspaper to carry to the picnic. When I was growing up, these ingredients often composed our Saturday night meal. We called it Supper Dish.

GRILLED VEGETABLE PACKETS

4 large potatoes, peeled and parboiled
1 large onion, sliced
½ pound fresh mushrooms, sliced
½ cup grated Parmesan cheese

8 slices bacon, crisply fried, drained and crumbled
salt and pepper to taste
½ cup butter or margarine

1. Cut six 9-inch squares of heavy-duty aluminum foil.

2. Slice potatoes and divide among the squares of foil. Add onion and mushroom slices and sprinkle with cheese and bacon. Salt and pepper to taste.

3. Cut butter into pats and lay on top of the vegetables.

4. Bring edges of foil up to enclose vegetables and seal packets following directions on page 34.

5. Place packets on grill over hot coals and cook 20 to 30 minutes, turning once halfway through the cooking time.

Serves 6

PICNIC NOTE: Cooking time for these handy packets is only 20 to 30 minutes if potatoes are parboiled. If time does not allow for parboiling, raw potatoes can be used, but the cooking time should be increased to 1 hour to ensure that potatoes are thoroughly cooked.

RATATOUILLE PIE

1 recipe Single Crust Pastry (page 188)	¼ cup finely shredded Jarlsberg or Gruyère cheese
2 cups Ratatouille (page 125), drained	3 eggs
	1 cup milk

1. Preheat oven to 425°F.

2. Prepare pastry according to directions on page 188. Roll out to a 12-inch circle on a lightly floured surface. Fit into a 9-inch pie plate. Trim overhang, turn under and flute edges and prick shell all over with a fork. Bake for 8 minutes. Remove and cool slightly.

3. Decrease oven temperature to 375°F.

4. Put half of Ratatouille in cooled pastry shell, then sprinkle with half the cheese. Repeat with remaining Ratatouille and cheese.

5. Beat eggs slightly, then beat in milk and pour mixture over the Ratatouille. Bake for 40 minutes or until center is almost set but still soft. Do not overbake. Custard will set as it cools. Let stand at least 15 minutes before serving.

6. ·Serve warm or cold as appetizer or entrée.

Serves 6 to 8

Variation: One pound thinly sliced Italian sweet sausage can be added to this dish for a meaty version. Simply add the sausage with the other ingredients to the pastry shell.

CRUNCHY CHICKEN VEGETABLE SALAD

Don't omit the peanuts. They add a special flavor and crunch to this tasty salad.

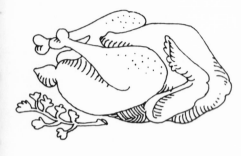

one 10¾-ounce can chicken broth	2 medium-size zucchini or cucumbers
5 cups water, or 4 cups water and 1 cup dry sherry	1½ teaspoons grated fresh ginger, or ½ teaspoon ground ginger
salt	1 clove garlic, minced
2 whole chicken breasts	½ teaspoon star anise (optional)
4 large carrots	1 tablespoon sherry
1 pound fresh green beans, or two 9-ounce packages frozen cut green beans	2 tablespoons honey
	½ cup soy sauce
4 scallions, or 1 small red onion, thinly sliced and broken into rings	½ cup peanut oil
	¼ cup chopped peanuts

1. In a medium-size saucepan, combine chicken broth and the water.

2. Lightly salt the chicken breasts and add to the broth. Bring to a boil, then reduce heat and simmer, covered, for 1 hour. Remove chicken and cool. Reserve cooking liquid for soup or sauces.

3. Peel carrots and cut into thin strips approximately 2 inches long. Cut ends of strips diagonally.

4. Cut green beans diagonally into pieces approximately 2 inches long.

5. Drop carrots and green beans into boiling salted water. Reduce heat and simmer 5 minutes only. Drain, rinse with ice water and chill immediately.

6. Cut scallions, including green tops, into thin rounds or prepare red onion as directed.

7. Quarter zucchini, then cut into long, thin strips.

8. Remove skin from cooled chicken. Remove meat from bones and cut meat into slivers.

9. In a large bowl, combine chicken slivers, chilled carrots and beans, scallions or red onions, and zucchini strips. Toss gently, cover and chill.

10. To make dressing, combine remaining ingredients except peanuts in a shaker jar and shake vigorously.

11. Garnish chilled salad with chopped peanuts and serve with dressing.

Serves 6 to 8

PICNIC NOTE: Carry chilled salad and prepared dressing to the picnic in separate containers. Toss with dressing just before serving. This salad is also good served over cold, cooked rice, especially Sushi Rice (page 47).

COUNTRY-STYLE BARBECUED SPARERIBS

country-style spareribs
   (thick, meaty cuts;
   allow two to three per
   person)
salt and pepper to taste

1   medium to large onion,
      finely chopped
Black Brandied Barbecue
      Sauce (page 192)

1. Preheat oven to 400°F.

2. To remove excess grease from ribs, place them in enough boiling water to cover them, reduce heat and simmer 15 minutes. Remove, drain and pat dry with paper towels.

3. Place ribs in a shallow baking dish, sprinkle with salt and pepper to taste and cover with chopped onion and Black Brandied Barbecue Sauce. Cover tightly with aluminum foil. Bake for 45 minutes, turning once. Remove from oven, cool slightly, and skim off any remaining grease.

4. Transfer ribs and sauce to a container with a tight-fitting lid.

5. At picnic site, lift ribs from the sauce and arrange on a grill over hot coals. Baste with barbecue sauce while grilling until ribs are nicely browned, about 15 minutes.

NOTE: If you'd like to use this recipe for non-picnic meals, remove the foil covering after the 45-minute baking period and bake an additional 15 minutes to brown the meat. Serve with barbecue sauce spooned over the ribs.

PICNIC NOTE: These ribs can also be completely cooked as noted above, then transferred to a preheated thermal container for a picnic where grills are not available. Be sure to pack plenty of napkins!

BAR-B-Q

2 pounds lean ground beef	1⅓ cups ketchup
1 tablespoon butter or margarine	2 tablespoons brown sugar
1 tablespoon lemon juice	1½ teaspoons dry mustard
2 tablespoons red wine vinegar	1 teaspoon salt
2 tablespoons brandy (optional)	1⅓ cups finely diced celery
¼ cup water	¼ cup finely chopped onion
	Homemade Burger Buns (page 123)

1. In a large heavy skillet, brown beef, stirring frequently to prevent lumping. Reduce heat and cover to keep warm.

2. In a medium-size saucepan, melt butter over medium heat and add lemon juice, vinegar, brandy (if desired), water and ketchup. Stir in sugar until dissolved, then add mustard and salt. Add celery and onion to sauce and heat thoroughly but do not cook so long that vegetables soften.

3. Drain any fat from the browned beef. Add sauce and vegetables to beef and mix well.

4. Serve on Homemade Burger Buns.

Serves 8

PICNIC NOTE: Carry this crunchy Bar-B-Q to your picnic in a wide-mouthed thermal container. Take along a big spoon or ladle to scoop it onto Burger Buns.

HUNGARIAN CORNUCOPIAS

one 8-ounce package cream cheese	2 anchovies, finely chopped
¼ cup butter or margarine	1 shallot, finely chopped
1 teaspoon capers	½ teaspoon caraway seed
1 teaspoon paprika	½ teaspoon salt
	thinly sliced ham or salami

1. Combine cream cheese and butter, and cream together. Add remaining ingredients except ham and mix well.

2. Spread on slices of ham and roll. Secure each roll with a toothpick. Cover and refrigerate until serving time.

Yield: 24 to 36 appetizers

Variation: Cheese mixture can be used to spread on crackers or fill raw mushroom caps.

SALMON COULIBIAC

This recipe is an updated version of a traditional Russian peasant pie. Normally wrapped in a yeast dough, this one is wrapped instead in a flaky cheese biscuit dough and can be served hot or cold.

one	16-ounce can salmon, drained and flaked with bones removed	1½	teaspoons salt
½	pound ground pork, veal or lamb	¼	teaspoon pepper
		1	teaspoon dried dill
¾	cup finely chopped onion	2	teaspoons parsley flakes
1	clove garlic, minced	1	cup fine dry bread crumbs
1	teaspoon Dijon-style mustard	2	eggs
½	teaspoon Worcestershire sauce	1	recipe Cheese Biscuits (page 60)
			sour cream (optional)

1. Preheat oven to 375°F.

2. In a large bowl, combine salmon and ground meat, and mix well. Blend in remaining ingredients except Cheese Biscuits. If mixture is too dry to hold together, add a little milk.

3. Place mixture in a lightly oiled 9 × 5-inch loaf pan and bake for 1 hour. Meanwhile, prepare Cheese Biscuit dough.

4. Remove baked salmon loaf from oven and increase oven temperature to 400°F.

5. After kneading the prepared biscuit dough, roll out to a rectangle large enough to line a 9 × 5-inch loaf pan and hang over the edges 1½ to 2 inches.

6. Carefully transfer cooked salmon loaf to biscuit-lined pan. Fold short ends of dough in over salmon loaf. Then fold in long edges; seal and crimp edges together. Bake for 20 to 25 minutes, until golden brown.

7. Slice and serve hot or cold with Mustard Mayonnaise (page 190) or with a dollop of sour cream.

Yield: nine 1-inch slices

HAM AND SPINACH "BOWS"

These meat-filled dough balls are a variation of a filled Chinese bun which is traditionally steamed. These are baked, however, and are good hot, cold or reheated. They can be baked ahead of time and frozen if you like.

one 1-pound loaf frozen bread dough	1 clove garlic, minced
1 pound fresh spinach, chopped and steamed, or one 10-ounce package frozen chopped spinach, cooked according to package directions and drained	2 cups ground or finely chopped cooked ham
	1 cup ricotta cheese
	¼ cup grated Parmesan cheese
	1 tablespoon dried dill, or 2 tablespoons minced fresh dill
1 small onion, chopped	2 to 3 tablespoons butter or margarine, melted

1. Remove loaf of dough from package and thaw as package directs until dough is pliable, about 1 to 2 hours.

2. Combine remaining ingredients except butter in a large bowl and mix well. Set aside.

3. With a lightly floured knife, cut the thawed loaf in half lengthwise and then cut each half into six pieces. Roll each piece of dough into a ball.

4. On a lightly floured surface, roll each ball into a circle approximately 6 inches in diameter.

5. Divide filling among dough circles, placing approximately 3 tablespoons of filling in the center of each one. Pull edges of dough up and around filling and seal by pinching together.

6. Place buns, sealed side down, on a greased baking sheet. Cover and let rise in a warm place for about 20 minutes or until puffy and light.

7. Preheat oven to 350°F.

8. Bake for 20 minutes or until golden brown.

9. Serve warm with hot Cheese Sauce (below), or at room temperature.

Serves 6

Variations: Any meat or vegetable filling can be used in place of the ham and spinach mixture. Try Bar-B-Q (page 206) lifted from its sauce with a slotted spoon to avoid sogginess. Texas Chili (page 172) is another tasty alternative.

CHEESE SAUCE

3   tablespoons butter or
        margarine
3   tablespoons all-purpose
        flour
1½   cups milk

1. In a medium saucepan, melt butter, then stir in flour and cook over low heat for 3 minutes. Add milk, stirring constantly to avoid lumping.

2. As soon as sauce starts to bubble, stir in the cheese, salt and pepper. Cook until cheese melts and the sauce is smooth, stirring constantly to avoid scorching.

Yield: about 2 cups sauce

SHISH KEBAB

This easy-to-fix skewer food is probably one of the most popular picnic dishes because of its built-in versatility. Ingredients can vary, based on what's seasonally available or according to the whim of each picnicker.

SHISH KEBAB INGREDIENTS

Meats and Seafoods	Vegetables	Fruits
London broil, cubed	cherry tomatoes or	pineapple chunks, fresh
smoked oysters wrapped	tomato wedges	or canned
in bacon	green pepper, cut into	spiced crab apples
lamb, cubed	1-inch squares	dates
shrimp	zucchini, cubed	apple chunks with skin
scallops	water chestnuts	papaya chunks
chicken, cubed	potato chunks, parboiled	banana chunks
cooked ham, cubed	mushrooms, whole or	(firm but ripe)
chicken livers, wrapped	caps	
in bacon	artichoke hearts	
chunks of hot dogs or	onions, parboiled	
sausages	eggplant chunks	
lobster chunks		

General Directions

1. Cut meats into 1½-inch chunks and marinate in your favorite marinade for several hours or overnight.

2. Prepare selected fruits and vegetables and place in separate containers.

3. **a.** At picnic site, arrange ingredients attractively on a serving platter and allow picnickers to design their own kebabs, choosing their favorite combinations.

    b. Or prepare skewers before packing and transport in the top of the picnic cooler. Be sure to carry extra meat marinade to brush skewered foods while they cook. Also consider threading each ingredient on separate skewers and grilling each the ideal amount of time to cook through. Fruits, mushrooms and tomatoes require the least cooking time, then meats and other vegetables. Timing will also vary according to the size of food chunks and the heat of the fire.

4. Space meat chunks on skewers close together for rare cooked meats, farther apart with open space all around for well-done meats.

5. Place skewers on grill over medium coals and cook 10 minutes, turning occasionally. Most meats, if cut into 1- to 1½-inch chunks, will cook in this amount of time. Long-cooking vegetables, unless parboiled or blanched, can take as long as 20 minutes. Quick-cooking foods require 3 to 5 minutes for optimum taste and texture.

RICE-IN-A-POUCH

Ideally, Shish Kebab should be served over pilaf, but that usually means carrying an extra pot and mixing utensils. With picnicking ingenuity you can lighten the load by cooking in two large sheets of heavy-duty aluminum foil. No pots to wash!

one 6-ounce package of your favorite packaged, seasoned, fast-cooking rice	butter, water and any other ingredients required in the package directions
	one 3-ounce can sliced mushrooms (optional)

1. Stack two 18-inch squares of heavy-duty aluminum foil and bring up the edges to form a pouch.

2. Put packaged rice ingredients, any additional required ingredients and mushrooms (if desired) in pouch. Stir carefully to mix and seal the pouch following directions on page 34.

3. Place on a grill over hot coals for 20 minutes.

4. Serve directly from the pouch or transfer to a serving bowl or individual plates.

Serves 6

SOUR CREAM FUDGE CAKE

½ cup butter or margarine	2½ teaspoons baking powder
1 cup sugar	
3 egg yolks, well beaten	two 1-ounce squares unsweetened chocolate, melted
3 egg whites, stiffly beaten	
½ cup dairy sour cream	
2 tablespoons milk	1 teaspoon vanilla
1½ cups all-purpose flour	1 recipe Fudge Icing (below)

1. Preheat oven to 350°F.

2. Cream butter and sugar together in a medium-size mixing bowl.

3. Add beaten egg yolks and mix well. Stir in beaten egg whites. Add sour cream and milk and mix well.

4. Sift flour and baking powder together and add to batter. Stir in melted chocolate and vanilla.

5. Spoon batter into a well-greased and floured 9-inch cake pan. Bake for 30 to 40 minutes or until toothpick inserted in center comes out clean. Cool in pan 10 minutes. Invert onto cake rack to cool.

6. Frost with Fudge Icing.

Serves 8

FUDGE ICING

2 cups sugar	¾ cup semisweet chocolate pieces
½ cup milk	
1 tablespoon butter or margarine	1 cup chopped walnuts
	1 teaspoon vanilla

1. Combine sugar, milk, butter and chocolate in a small saucepan. Bring to a boil, stirring constantly. Reduce heat and cook for 8 minutes.

2. Remove from heat and beat until creamy. Stir in walnuts and vanilla just before icing thickens.

3. *Pour immediately* over the cake and leave to harden. Do not try to spread on the cake.

Yield: about 2½ cups

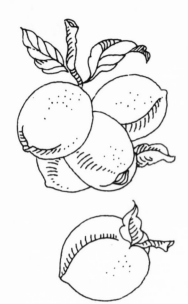

FRESH PEACH SUGAR CRUMB PIE

Children love this sugary pastry baked in small tart pans. For an alcoholic version, prepare the peaches before making the sugar crumb crust and sprinkle them with a little brandy.

¼	cup butter	½	teaspoon cinnamon
½	cup sugar	6	small to medium-size
½	cup light brown sugar, firmly packed		fresh peaches, peeled, pitted and sliced
1	cup all-purpose flour		
¼	cup finely chopped almonds or hazelnuts		

1. Preheat oven to 350°F.

2. Cream butter and sugars together. Add remaining ingredients except peaches and mix thoroughly.

3. Pat half of the mixture into the bottom of a 9-inch pie plate or divide half of it among several small tart pans.

4. Arrange peach slices on top of the crumb crust.

5. Cover fruit with the remaining crumbs. Bake for 45 to 60 minutes, until lightly browned.

Serves 6

Variations: Any fresh fruit or combination can be substituted for fresh peaches. Or try Friendship Fruit (page 175) for a spicy alternative. If you're in a real hurry, substitute a large can of sliced peaches, drained, for the fresh fruit.

BRANDIED DATE NUT SAUCE

This is wonderful over fresh homemade ice cream or pound cake.

2	cups light brown sugar, packed	one	8-ounce package whole or chopped dates
1	cup water	1	cup coarsely chopped walnuts or pecans
¼	cup brandy		

1. In a medium-size saucepan, cook sugar and water together over medium heat to make a syrup. Cook for 20 minutes, stirring occasionally.

2. Add brandy, dates and nuts, and mix thoroughly. Allow to cool, then transfer to a glass jar with lid. Allow to stand at least 2 days before serving.

3. Serve at room temperature, or warmed, over ice cream, cake or crêpes.

Yield: about 1½ cups

INDEX